POLITICS OF THE
ARCHAIC PELOPONNESE

POLITICS

OF THE

ARCHAIC
PELOPONNESE

The transition from Archaic to Classical politics

K. Adshead

AN AVEBURY MONOGRAPH

First published in 1986 by Avebury Publishing Company.
© K. Adshead, 1986. All rights reserved.

Available from:
Gower Publishing Company Limited
Gower House
Croft Road
Aldershot
Hampshire GU11 3HR
England

and

Gower Publishing Company
Old Post Road
Brookfield
Vermont 05036
USA

British Library Cataloguing in Publication Data:

Adshead, K.
  Politics of the Archaic Peloponnese.
  1. Peloponnesus (Greece) — Politics and
  government   2. Greece — Politics and
  government — To 146 B.C.
  I. Title
  320.938   DF261.P3

  ISBN 0—86127—024—X

Printed in Great Britain by Blackmore Press,
Longmead, Shaftesbury, Dorset.

TABLE OF CONTENTS

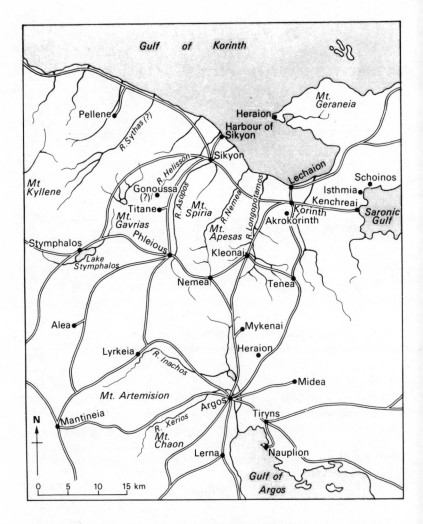

Map of the Northeast Peloponnese (derived from Roux, *Pausanias en Corinthie*).
Reproduced with the kind permission of Clarendon Press, Oxford.

Chapter 1

THE FRAMEWORK OF
THE NORTHEAST PELOPONNESE

The northeast Peloponnese is geographically unified by the communications network running north-south through it. For the geographical zone thus created, there were in the Archaic and early Classical period two political options open: unified politically, the area might become a regional power of the first rank, hegemon of central Greece and the coastal water-ways on either side: or else, disunited, it might become merely the fragmented landbridge between superpowers, strategically significant for them but in itself lacking influence.

The present essay is concerned with the factors that in two decades determined the decision for the second option. Prior, however, to a discussion of political developments, the framework of potential provided by human geography should be set out. For it is this framework of highway and byway that is throughout the underlying explanatory factor. It provides the context in which Corinth, Argos and the Arcadian cities confront one another. Had they been arranged differently on the physical map, the drama must have been other than it was.[1]

The political possibility of union is the product of the topography of roads. To begin a history of the northeast with the communications network that guarantees its unity is to break new ground. For the area is more than the sum of its conventional parts, viz. Corinthia, Argolis, Arcadia, Akte. The region was seldom perceived as one, even geographically. True, ancient usage occasionally employed 'Argos' or 'Argeia' for the northeast zone in its entirety, but in general these

1

terms meant either the city of Argos or the Argolic plain alone. The ancient geographers, Strabo and Pausanias, considered the district in terms of a series of broken journeys from point to point, although Strabo's itinerary is the more cohesive, with its emphasis on relative distances and interlocking vantage points. To insist therefore on the functional unity of the northeast Peloponnese in virtue of the strategic highway upon which it hinges is more novel than the familiar groupings of its several cities might suggest.[2]

The communications system of the northeast Peloponnese

The communications system begins with Corinth and ends with Tegea on the frontiers of Laconia. It is defined by such cities and towns as lie on the main road (Corinth, Tenea, Cleonae, Argos and Tegea) and also by those settlements that control the side roads: (Sicyon, Phlius, Nemea and Mantinea). Most ancient cities of the northeast come into this bracket; those that do not are principally the settlements of the Akte and southeast Argolis, to a lesser extent the western sites, Sicyon and Phlius. Their lack of relation to the all-important corridor consigned them, during the Classical period, to relative insignificance. The core of the region, then, is the Corinth-Tegea road in its fullest extension, a land bridge, a couloir; 'an axis of history' in Fernand Braudel's memorable phrase.[3] Correspondingly in setting out the cities and towns of the region, it must be their status vis-à-vis the road that is emphasised.

Corinth.[4] 'Corinth on two seas' is proverbial. Corinth as the junction of Peloponnesian communications should be equally so: 'Die Lage der Stadt Korinth i.A. war...durchaus geeignet zur Beherrschung des Landverkehrs'.[5] It was control of all the southern approaches to the Isthmus of Corinth which, with the impregnable Acrocorinth, made the city chief of the 'Fetters of Greece'. Control of the coast road from Sicyon complemented her hold on the main northsouth artery. The accoutrements of the fifth century hoplite exacerbated this grip on troop movements, for even if a northwardbound Spartan host detoured with great difficulty to the West (Sicyon) to avoid the main highway, still they must pass in

2

the end under the walls of Corinth and not only that, must so pass with right flank exposed to the city walls. The Long Walls, built ca. 460 B.C. did no more than re-affirm the city's strategic advantages and Mt. Oneion, opposite Acrocorinth, completed Corinth's hold on the corridor entrance.

As if her location at the hub of the ancient roads was not enough, Corinth had an acropolis of unusual scale to ensure the exploitation of her position. Strabo's enthusiastic account deserves to be read in this light for he appreciated the significance of fortified citadels and of observation posts with an extensive coverage of the surrounding terrain. Excavations on the summit of Acrocorinth suggest a watchman's outpost may have been sited in the southeast corner, comparable to that on the Larisa at Argos and there may also have been another lookout on the East Hill, within the east city wall. It is significant that communications between Corinth and Tenea, the first important station on the highway, ran not only from the city but from the Teneatic Gate on the northwest slopes: a garrison at Tenea would be in close contact with city and acropolis and it would not be 'hill travellers' so much as scouts and soldiers who used the more direct hill path now found to run via Mapsos due south over the hills to Chiliomodion. Below the citadel, on the first slopes of the rise, lay the Phliasian Gate, which Pritchett suggests is the main point of entry from the south. For travellers, perhaps: but ancient armies going north will have bypassed the city proper and proceeded past Tenea and then (again with exposed right flank) past Mt Oneion, long fortified by the Corinthians. The northwest prospect towards Sicyon was less important in that the way north through Arcadia and then east was always secondary: but still the Phliasian Gate and Acrocorinth were linked inside the circuit of the walls and there was a clear view to the gates of old Sicyon. Like the Argives, the Corinthians exploited from the first the military and political potential afforded by their situation at a nodal point in the system.[6]

Tenea.[7] Seven miles on from Corinth near the modern Chiliomodion stood Tenea, a place visited by both Pausanias and Strabo, now however nothing but masonry crumbling in the sun. The authors of *Corinth* III, pt. 1 note that it must have been important once to justify the special description the travellers award it, but they seem at a loss to say in what this importance lay: an inland town, a fortified outpost, a wayfarer's rest, or as they indicate, the start of a narrow alternative hill path to the Argolid, used by Agesilaus in 393 B.C. and identified by H. G. Lolling with the hill track or Kontoporeia mentioned by Polybius and Athenaeus.[8] If now the opening remarks of the present chapter are taken into account, the full importance of Tenea's situation may be seen. In the first place, armies bypassing the city of Corinth took this, the flatter, easier way; in the second place, while the road Tenea-Argolis via Ayionorion was not a good one, it had strategic value as a bypass. The close relation between function in the roads system and the character of a settlement could not be more clearly seen. Without this appreciation, however, there is a temptation to give Tenea some political or religious raison d'être, whence the perpetuation in every handbook of an oracular comment by Apollo, 'εὐδαίμων ὁ Κορίνθος, ἐγὼ δ᾽ εἴην Τενεάτης',[9] supposedly suggesting some peculiar peaceful charm about the village. Tenea's function was to control the side road, up past the spring of Ayionorion to Limnai and so out into the Argive plain two and a half miles southeast of the Heraion, four and a half miles southeast of Mycenae. The descent from Ayionorion to Limnai is steep and difficult, therefore the strategic potential meagre. Tenea's role therefore was that of insurance against a surprise attack.

Cleonae.[10] The arterial north-south route turned west from Tenea and from following the valley of the Leukon river, headed west, for the upper basin of the parallel but more westerly Longopotamos, skirting the northward slopes of the massif till the divide between the twin peaks of Mt Tretos made a southerly direction feasible. The upper basin of the Longopotamos was the plain of Cleonae, a city which not only sat beside the road to the south over the pass, but also astride the only east-west outlet along the couloir, the route to Nemea, Phlius, and the west. It is at this point only in the central stretch of the route system that there is a significant east-west linkage: from Corinth in the north, Argos in the centre, or Tegea in the south, lesser branches might run either east, west or southwest as the case might be, but along the main north-south segment of the highway the vista

4

narrowed and, Cleonae-Nemea-Phlius apart, there was no major east-west axis to redirect the pressures of the cities to north and south of the corridor. Both Leake and Philippson draw attention to the Cleonae road west as a break in the east Arcadian highlands. Philippson writes of 'der i.A. wichtigen Strasse von Kleonai nach Pheneós';[11] similarly Leake calls it, 'a road of considerable traffic leading from Anápli, Argos and Corinth to Foniá, [Pheneus] Kalávyrta and Patra.'[12] Noticeably absent from both itineraries, however, is any significant southern feed-in from central or southern Arcadia over the Saïtas watershed, and without this southern connection no general importance can be assigned to the westward axis.

Cleonae was visible from Corinth, was nearer Corinth than Argos, only 80 stades (20 km) from the former, 120 (30 km) from the latter. She therefore leaned on Argos to protect her from the greater danger Corinth, a policy which avoided one takeover only to be forced into another. This illustrates a peculiarity of the northeast Peloponnesian couloir, for in similar corridors, the Brenner pass over the Alps for example, Innsbruck in the center, not Verona to the south or Munich to the north, has been the political key to the area. In the couloir from Corinth to Tegea the midway sites, Nemea, Cleonae, Mycenae made only abortive attempts in classical times to assert themselves against the greater cities to the north and south.

Cleonae also controlled the by-route traditionally identified with the Kontoporeia which, like the track from Tenea by Ayionorion, went over the Arakhnaion massif direct without swerving west in search of a lower pass. Starting from Hagios Basileios, this was another 'series of toilsome zig-zags'[13] between Mts Daphnis and Kutulion to Guni and then, skirting the northern slopes of Mt Elias, down on to the Argolic plain at Mycenae. Neither track was appealing, being steep and dry as were most overhill tracks, to judge by the stress the itineraries lay on the infrequent springs or streams along their course. The ancient world persisted in believing that Cleonae was an archetypal case of vanished glories. 'I flinch from showing you Cleonae', says Lucian's Charon, 'for cities like ourselves are moribund.'[14] In fact its modest but real status as guardian of the crossroads seems to have remained unusually steady.

Nemea.[15] Westwards from Cleonae two and a half miles lies Nemea, higher than Cleonae, a valley two and a half by three-quarters of a mile wide, through which flows the river Nemea. Like Cleonae and Phlius on either side, Nemea's importance derived from its position on the one westward axis off the highway. Unlike Cleonae and Phlius, it had no outlet to the north, for the basin in which it is situated ends in a marshland whereas the Longopotamos on the east and Asopus on the west issue out through narrow ravines to the plain of Corinth. In terms of network, therefore, Nemea was simply a stage between Cleonae and Phlius and this functional insignificance is reflected in the fact that the site was unfortified.

Two aspects of Nemea's situation in the communication system of the northeast may be elaborated. First is the ambiguity of its adherence: plainly it was a satellite but whose? Cleonae and after her, Argos, maintained their influence by force of arms, finally fortifying the pass between Nemea and Phlius with the fort Trikaranon. On the other hand there was the natural tendency of one mountain polis to side with another against the lowlands; the association of Phlius and Nemea was expressed in literature as early as Pindar, who wrote of Nemea as 'δασκίοις / Φλιοῦντος ὑπ' ὠγυγίοις ὄρεσιν.'[16] Nemea lay in a transitional zone between northern Arcadia and the northeast: had communication to the west been better, more effort might have been made by Phlius or another Arcadian state to take over Nemea whenever Cleonae or Argos seemed vulnerable.

Secondly, from Nemea southeast ran two roads into the Argive plain: beginning together they ran south for a short distance but then diverged. The more northerly of the two (Thucydides' ὄρθιος ἕτερα) came around Megalovouno via Milioti to Phichtion, opposite Mycenae. The more southerly χαλεπὴ ὁδός went via Malandrenion into the Inachus valley. The former of these routes (also called the Kelossa approaches by Xenophon) was in regular use till recent years, the latter, however, a difficult road in 418 B.C., has been discarded. Both roads have traces of ancient watch towers at key points, especially on the Kelossa road where the fourth century in particular saw the construction of a series of interlocking towers and walls. The opportunity for a double or triple descent on Argos from the north was thus uniquely afforded

6

by Nemea, and an army which wished to undertake this manoeuvre would first group at Phlius and then divide at Nemea before attacking.[17]

Phlius.[18] The role of Phlius on the axis west from the main route is similar to Nemea's. A difference is that more side routes open in other directions, e.g. north to Sicyon, southeast to Orneae, southwest to Mantinea and Orchomenus. Phlius lay on a ridge running, significantly, east-west, open on three sides to the plain and high above the surrounding landscape: from here the whole of the Phliasian plain was visible. The upper terraces of the ridge formed the ancient acropolis. The acropolis of Phlius was well walled, some of the east tower stands today.

It is important for the argument to establish that there was no easy connection, no convenient link-up between the east-west route (Cleonae-Phlius) and the Mantiniké in central Arcadia, to the southwest. For much has been made of Phlius' importance as an assembly point for the Peloponnesian League. It will be argued that the various campaigns in which Phlius was so used by Sparta, coming north via Tegea and Mantinea past Orchomenus, do not give this estimate of Phlius' worth much support. More, it is intended to show what these routes south and southwest from Phlius were like and to contrast them with the axial highway eastwest, Phlius-Nemea-Cleonae, already described, and also with the useful but scarcely comfortable road north from Phlius to Sicyon. There *is* a modern road under construction from Levidi in the southwest of central Arcadia to Kandila and so to Skotini/Psarion (with a sharp turn east down into the Phliasian plain). Meyer traversed this pass from Kandila in 1937 calling it an 'Anstieg...durch eine grossartig wilde, tief eingerissene Schlucht.'[19] This however is not the way that antiquity knew, the mountain road from Kandila over Mt Oligyrton to Stymphalia and only then east to Phlius. This road, Pausanias' road, was so arduous and lengthy as to constitute no real alternative to the main network, suitable only for an emergency escape or surprise attack, slow and risky at best. The descent from Kandila to Stymphalos down Lykorrheuma (Wolf's Ravine) was so steep that riders in Frazer's day went one abreast down the precipitous bridle path.

Frazer's account is graphic:

7

We are following the path to Stymphalus which, leaving the village of Kandyla in a northerly direction, ascends the mountains by zigzags along the edge of precipices. The snow sometimes lies here as late as March making the ascent difficult and dangerous... We reach the first *col* or summit of the pass about an hour and twenty minutes from Kandyla...Half an hour more takes us to a second *col* or summit,...The way now goes down a ravine shut in on both sides by lofty fir clad mountains and known as the Wolf's Ravine (*Lykorrheuma*) from the wolves that are said to abound in it. Thus descending we reach the valley of Stymphalus and the western end of the lake.[20]

'Am stärksten ist Arkadia abgesperrt auf der Nordseite', writes Philippson in his preliminary *Übersicht*:[21] this is the crucial factor in the elimination of other north-south routes through the Peloponnese besides the main Corinth-Argos artery. Not only is the mountainous terrain a deterrent but the backward tilting of the conglomerate has produced an unusual drainage pattern of unpredictable marshlands and disappearing lakes which has also impeded transit. Much of Arcadia is in perpetual danger of being waterlogged anyway ('the danger is surfeit, not scarcity, of water') relieved only by the famous *katavothra*, which were not as well maintained in the Orchomenia as further south. To these obstacles was added the difficulty of the pass itself: in the circumstances Busolt and Pritchett's enthusiasm for Phlius as the nodal point of an alternative trans-Arcadian system is hard to understand.[22]

It would also be possible to go from Mantinea to Phlius, skirting Argive territory, if one took the more northern of the two paths from Mantinea to the Argolid, the so called Climax ('ladder'), with its summit between Sangas and Kaparelion, and then upon following the Inachos valley downwards again struck up into the mountains east of Malandrenion and so over to Nemea. Today this is a footpath only and from the steepness of the grade must always have been so desperate a route as to deter all but the most foolhardy general. It is plainly very difficult to get from the north of Lakonia through to Phlius across country, whether via the Mantiniké or the Argolid; this observation must reduce the value of Phlius' position and enhance that of the main highway.[23]

It remains to add that there is little to be said for the Phlius-Sicyon route either. It brings an army going north out on to the plain of Corinth with its right flank exposed, and (as has been mentioned) to leave the Peloponnese, Corinth must still be passed, on the right of a marching army. In itself the route, while better than the difficult itinerary from Mantinea to Phlius, still presented hazards. It ran from Phlius past Titane along the left (west) bank of the Asopus, to the shore, then east to Corinth, there was also the more direct way first along the east bank via ancient Thyamia and then over the foothills, going from the 'Corinthian Gate' on the acropolis of Phlius to the 'Phliasian Gate' of Corinth. It must be noted that the valley of the Asopos is steep and narrow and the path by no means secure from the river's reaches either. Roux writes: 'L'Asopos coule dans une vallée si étroitement encaissée, si souvent recoupée par les lits des torrents qu'elle ne facilite pas les communications entre les deux pays.'[24] The section of the route over the foothills was little better; having crossed the ridge of Mt Evangelistria (Spiria) it descended into the valley of the Nemea only to rise again over the foothills of Mt Apesas and so reach the west wall of Corinth. An army taking this route would be slightly less exposed to flank attack, though what it gained in defence it would have lost in difficulty of transport and loss of time. All in all the whole conception of an alternative north-south network pivoting on Phlius should be abandoned.

Mycenae.[25] Returning then from this discussion of the east-west side road, the next major site upon the arterial highway is Mycenae whose position midway between Corinth and Argos clearly deserves analysis in the idiom of routes. Situated off the road to the east on another impressive natural acropolis, Mycenae has a baffling history upon which consideration of its situation in a regional communication network sheds only a little extra light. Its rise in Helladic times is as dark as the exact circumstances of its destruction in the fifth century. In the debate on the origins of the Mycenaeans, their relations with the Minoans, the character of their society, it is surprising how little the question: 'Why this site, of all the mid-bronze age sites?' has been raised. A token remark about roadways radiating northwest and south, backed by reference to Captain Steffen's maps — that is all, the issue is considered closed. Similarly when Mycenae was finally destroyed it was because, according to Diodorus, the

Spartans, allies of Mycenae, were preoccupied with internal troubles and could not relieve the siege laid by Cleonae and Argos.[26] But what can Mycenae be doing as a Spartan satellite, sited as she is on the far side of Argos from Sparta? Why did Cleonae take the part of Argos, yet afterwards accept part of the exiled vanquished? Did Mycenae really seek a revival of her ancient hegemony — as her claim to hold the Nemean Games might suggest? Mycenae's history remains enigmatic.

The city guards the southern outlet of the pass of Dervenaki and also the outlet for the Kelossa approaches, one of the possible routes from Phlius southeast out on to the Argive plain. On the summit of Mt Elias are the remains of Mycenae's watchtowers signifying that she did indeed exercise the potential control of the mountain bloc that nature afforded her. Captain Steffen's roads showed a definite northward orientation, in fact they were the three roads of historic times, the main highway, the Kontoporeia, and the Nemean hill route. Mycenae was a foothills state and her early power rested on the control of mountain passes. We may compare as before the situation of Innsbruck, holding her own vis-à-vis Verona and Munich, south and north of her, or Roman Lugdunum, another city in the centre of a land isthmus, with Trier to the north and Marseilles to the south.[27]

Historical geography, however, only provides the possibilities which may or may not be realised, and that intermittently: geographical determinism is the last thesis of its dogmatic. Several sets of circumstances may contribute to the decline of a mid-isthmus power: its chances are related to the strength or weakness of one or both termini; also it may itself mutate so as to dilute the essential raison d'être of its ascendancy.

We may see both these circumstances operating at the two moments of Mycenae's history under discussion. For example in the great days of LH III A–B, Corinth was relatively retarded, while north of the Isthmus of Corinth, Athens, though substantial, was still more provincial than Mycenae. To the south, Sparta, perhaps more prosperous, still seems weak in relation to her later development. Corinth, Athens, or Sparta in the ascendant would at once alter Mycenae's importance. Second, the plain of Argos falling under Mycenae's sway, effected a basic change in the character of the Mycenaean state itself, re-orienting it towards the plain in the south and diluting that virtue of location to which it owed its rise: instead a new zone came into being, the Argolid, with its capital at Argos. We may compare the case of the mountain kingdom of Savoy which, spreading out into the North Italic plain, dissipated its own strength in the course of producing the greater unit, Italy itself. Later on, Mycenae fell to Argos and Cleonae (however this actually happened in 468 B.C.); the power and strength of the two termini beyond the Isthmus, Athens and Sparta, operated as contributing factors. With these two great centers attracting events out toward them it was difficult to imagine Mycenae's bid to become once again a key mountain state, mistress of the passes, succeeding even briefly. Mycenae then could only be the Argive outpost at the entrance to the plain of Argos.[28]

Argos.[29] Argos had from the first a national role as chief city of the plainland of the Argolid, 'der natürliche Mittelpunkt der Ebene'[30] and in addition she commanded the important swing to the west which the main highway has to make, over the low (700 m) saddle between Parnon and southeast Arcadia into the basin of Tegea, now eclipsed by Tripolis. 'Dès les temps des Atrides, cette plaine fut un centre de civilisation et de puissance politique, non seulement par ses moissons mais surtout parce qu'elle ouvre un accès vers le golfe de Corinthe et l'Arcadie.'[31] This sharp bend west was of greater strategic importance than is sometimes recognised. For example, the early Helladic site of Lerna, built on an earlier Neolithic settlement, was unmistakably fortified and equally unmistakably attacked and burned only to be rebuilt, burned down again and yet again rebuilt and this time refortified. 'There is no doubt that enemies came to Lerna.'[32] The violence of the overthrow of the EH II settlement is so striking that it obscures what must have been among the underlying causes of the struggle, namely possession of the narrow turn from the Argolid into southeastern Arcadia. Again and again in Peloponnesian history this area sees the thrust and counter-thrust of Peloponnesian powers being played out; Hysiae, the Battle of the Champions, and, as a dramatization of the importance of the site, Cleomenes' march up to the banks of the Erasinus river in 494 B.C., when the failure to obtain a propitious sacrifice may be rationalized as a reluctance to engage in a prolonged campaign in the Argolid without having fought it out first with the border garrison stationed at such places as Hysiae and Cenchreae further north. Argos' hold on this important bend was her primary advantage over and above the fact of her own rich territories. The fact that the acropolis lies between the old town and the main road, and the relatively more westward aspect of the old town than the new, are additional indications of this orientation towards the highway.

Second, Argos controlled the axial road east which might be held to challenge the claim of the Cleonae-Nemea-Phlius road to be the only west-east articulation of the central section of the highway. But the road to Tiryns, Nauplion, and Epidaurus, with its eastern extension to Hermione, was of even less strategic importance than the road to Phlius. The hinterland of Hermione and Epidaurus is a chalky plateau which rises in the Arakhnaion mountains to 3,629 feet, 'little better than a stony waterless wilderness',[33] from which or to which no host in history ever came. On the subject of the road network to the east of Argos today, the authors of the *Géographie Universelle* say 'le commerce ne l'utilise plus guère parce qu'elle confine à un desert. En effet, l'intérieur est un causse des plus pauvres et l'on n'y recontre guère que les troupeaux transhumants de l'Arcadie.'[34] Only the earliest stage of the road, the short stretch from Argos to Nauplion, proved its strategic significance in 494 B.C. when Cleomenes used it for his surprise attack. Even here it does not, properly speaking, form part of an important road network, for the Spartan troops made the first part of their journey by sea, and it was in this seaborne attack that the element of surprise (and so of success) lay. Ordinarily the Argos-Nauplion segment was as purely local in its significance as the rest of this particular axial link.

As Corinth armed Tenea on the other side of the highway from Acrocorinth to be the strongest point in a control system over the northern exit of the highway, so Argos constructed a system of forts fanning out round the western periphery of the Argolic plain, where the mountain tracks Climax and Prinus issue out into the valleys. Gschnitzer discusses the identification of forts like Orneae as a separate constitutional group distinct both from Mycenae and Tiryns and from the Argive serf colonists round Argos itself.[35] But it is the geographical context explanatory of these distinctions that should have attracted attention: the western

12

forts had the crucial task of holding down the western access to the highway, the vulnerable linkage — none was 'simply a fortified site in Argive territory' but rather a key to Argos' continuing political survival.

Tegea.[36] Tegea is the end of the classical highway, whereas the modern road and railway, essentially obeying the same geographico-political imperatives, go on for a distance of 59 miles before reaching the sea at Kalamata. Why is there this difference in termini? First, while Messenia today as before is a major division of the Peloponnese, it is now an independent nome with its own capital at Kalamata: in classical times however, after the first Messenian war (late eighth century), it was not independent but was ruled firmly from Sparta, despite the rebellions of the seventh and sixth centuries. Thus beyond Tegea, to southwest as well as southeast, lay only Laconia and her dependencies. Tegea was the beginning of the world beyond Sparta for the Spartans, the beginning of the strange and alien world of Sparta for the traveller from the north.

This point was further underlined by Sparta's sixth century decision to bring her policy of direct annexation to an end at the Tegeate frontier, and reinforced by the peculiar character of the Lycurgan regime which, whatever it permitted in the early sixth century, must towards the close of that century have embarked on the anti-mercantilist policy which tradition saw as among its more outstanding characteristics: 'of the moneymaking that depends on troublesome going and seeing people and doing business, they had no need at all'.[37] When this was combined with a notorious and persistent xenophobia, it is easy to see why the main communications network of the northern Peloponnese faltered and came to a standstill on the border between Tegea and Laconia.

Were there not other directions out of Tegea besides the southern exits? The road north to Mantinea was less important than it might have been: it ended, it is argued throughout this chapter, at Orchomenos to all intents and purposes, and never constituted an alternative but rather a 'feed-in' to the main system. The road northwest along the east foot of Mt Mainalos, leading to Vytina, the upper Ladon and so ultimately into Elis, was more arduous than the (longer) western route to and from Elis through Messenia, which the Eleans, usually allies of Sparta, were more likely to take.

Tegea then is the end of one major route and the beginning of other and minor routes in different directions unassociated with each other. After it there was no one broad highway for the commercial or military interests of adjacent city states to claim for themselves and to deny to others.

Mantinea.[38] Mantinea was 13 miles north of Tegea, in a marshy plain that lies below that of the southern city; the endless dispute over the regulation of the water from south to north is a leitmotiv of Mantinean history. Tegea's enemies tended to be Mantinea's friends, and vice versa, though the advent of ideological politics briefly interrupted this alternation.

Mantinea thus assumed a certain military importance for an army that needed a friendly base in Arcadia against Sparta. However, the roads that led from the north into Mantinea were negligible except in an emergency, when they might be worth a try. These roads have attracted a disproportionate amount of space from the early travellers. As argued earlier, neither the famous 'Ladder' route via Sangas, nor the more southerly 'Prinus route' via Karya from Mantinea onto the Argive plain was in serious use.[39] Only the southern road to Tegea was in any sense a highway, and then only an auxiliary to the major network which is the subject of this chapter.

With this sketch of the directional possibilities of Mantinea our survey of the main internal road from Corinth to Tegea with its traverses and cross-country potentialities is completed. The importance of Corinth to the north and Argos to the south emerges all the more strongly when the communications network is exhibited in full. The weakness of the road from Sicyon to Corinth, the fading out of the east-west axis from Cleonae to Phlius, the strategic monopoly of the saddle from Argos to Tegea add up to a denial that there was any other viable way out or into the Peloponnese except that which was so firmly held down by Corinth and Argos.

Historical examples

By way of an excursus to this general account, there follows

14

in the present section a survey of those historical occasions when an alternative to the main highway was attempted by a Greek army Peloponnesian or mainland. It will be surprisingly clear that these alternative marches met with minimal success. There are, thanks to the varying metaphysics of the ancient authors, an assortment of reasons for the ineffectiveness of these campaigns, none of which explicitly attempts a logistic approach. Nonetheless it may be suspected that the real reason for failure was in fact the difficulty of the going in dry, unfamiliar, and mountainous terrain, the endless bridle paths seldom used and little known;[40] and this conclusion can only highlight the importance of the one throughway which was (relatively) broad, commodious and in general use.

The three expeditions of the Spartans and their allies beyond the Peloponnese in the last years of the sixth century (512–506 B.C.) were collectively a failure even though individual campaigns (notably Cleomenes' expulsion of the Peisistratids in 510 B.C.) were successful. Busolt analyses the political opposition the Peloponnesian allies of Sparta felt to the extension of operations beyond the Peloponnese, and his basically diplomatic interpretation concludes 'die bisherigen Versuche der peloponnesischen Vormacht auch ausserhalb des Peloponnesos eine dominierende Stellung zu gewinnen, waren also durchgehends gescheitert.'[41] It is hard not to feel that the situation of Argos, controlling so large a sector of the route, influenced events, especially as Argos supported the Peisistratids. For example, Corinth easily called a halt to the final sortie, indicating a general lack of enthusiasm on the part of the allies, who feared perhaps that their way home would be obstructed.[42]

This threat from Argos was reduced for two decades from 494 B.C. by the great victory of Cleomenes at Sepeia.[43] Three points may be made about this battle which prove how close was the control of the highway by Argos. First, though Cleomenes evidently got through the frontier guards at Hysiae and Cenchreae, yet he turned back at the river Erasinus, ostensibly because the omens were unpropitious. Instead he assembled (from Aegina and Sicyon, surely a laborious effort) a small armada and ferried his army across to Asine, thus marching on Argos from the east. It may be inferred, first that he could not advance without first defeating the outposts, second that Argos' control of her territory was so complete as to discourage a thrust into the Argive plain even from the banks of the Erasinus. Secondly, Cleomenes' march on Argos from the east is in fact a rare instance of the lateral route, east-west, Nauplion-Argos, being used by an army. The fact that the area fell to Cleomenes so easily suggests that it was little used as a highway and thus was inadequately guarded, in contrast to the western road. Finally, after the battle, in Cleomenes' surprising failure to take Argos itself, we meet for the first but not the last time the curious phenomenon of armies that successfully get within reach of Argos suddenly pulling out and withdrawing from the area, their mission incomplete, snatching defeat from the jaws of victory. Busolt appears unsure of the reasons for Cleomenes' withdrawal, 'wie dem auch sein mag',[44] inclining however to the view that Cleomenes disliked the prospect of a long siege of Argos in the face of a resolute and uncompromising enemy. Thus he too implies that Argos held down her strategically sited territorium in an iron grip, and that reinforcements and supplies from north and south could not arrive because the only approaches were in hostile hands. Sepeia is therefore an interesting campaign from the insights into regional communications which it offers. It also had the effect, as Grote saw, of nullifying Argive medism in the hour of Greece's greatest danger. Without it the Spartan host would presumably have been even more dilatory in marching north out of the Peloponnese.

While the Thirty Years' Peace between Argos and Sparta was in force, 452/1–422/1 B.C., Sparta was able to move freely beyond the Isthmus, hence the relentless annual raids on Attica which caused so much suffering to the Athenians. After this freedom was removed in 422/1 B.C., it is clear that the subsequent eruption of hostilities meant Sparta could no longer go north so easily, instead in 413 B.C. she garrisoned Decelea and supplied it locally by raids on Attic soil. But the clearest evidence of the importance of the arterial highway comes earlier in Agis' Argive campaign of 418 B.C.[45] Agis wanted to compensate for the lapse of the treaty by a second Sepeia. The account of the battle of Mantinea given in Thucydides has been extensively criticised but the account of Agis' earlier Argive campaign has been little studied.

Critics have praised Agis' daring route marches and

excoriated the Argive sentries who let them pass unnoticed, first on the route from Methydrion to Mantinea, and secondly on their triple manoeuvre from Nemea; down into the Argive plain (1) via the main road, (2) the Kelossa approaches and finally (3) by the precipitous route down the Inachus valley below Orneae, the lower stages of the Climax route. These two itineraries, from Methydrion via Mantinea to Phlius, and from Phlius to Orneai, not easy at any time, will have been hazardous in the extreme by night. On the first leg, Methydrion-Mantinea-Phlius, little used, waterless mountain passes will have succeeded each other for most of the 40-mile distance and, given the need for haste, there were probably no pack animals at all on the steep tracks, thus the state of Agis' army, despite Thucydides' enthusiasm, cannot have been very encouraging. To follow this arduous night march by another equally taxing one down into the Argolid was to court the stalemate that Agis in fact achieved. His manoeuvres all worked to the extent that the Argives were unprepared for them. Only the army taking the Tretus pass failed to appear on time. Agis himself and the right wing were within striking distance of Argos: but what was the issue? An ignominious withdrawal, no battle whatever, Agis' house confiscated, himself fined. The obvious explanation is the exhaustion of Agis' troops, not the delay of the left wing or the absence of the Athenians. The bulk of the army arrived on time, bypassing the expected route (namely the main road), but to what end? When in position they could not fight. The absence of viable alternatives to the main highway was never more clearly revealed.

Campaigns in the fourth century show the same phenomenon. The Corinthian War was fought by the masters of the highway against Sparta and its effect was to immobilize Lacedaemon completely. The battle near the Nemea River (July 394 B.C.) illustrates the futility of alternative routes in two ways. First, the actual battle: the advance of Sparta through Arcadia to Sicyon, that is via Mantinea, Orchomenus and Phlius, was a hard march, through bad country, as has been argued: once debouching on to the coastal plain at Epieikeia whom should the Spartan force find awaiting them on their unprotected right but the peltasts of the opposing side. As the day wore on the Spartans, according to Xenophon, were hampered by the awkwardness of the terrain — the foothills of the limestone range of eastern Arcadia. The victory of the Spartans was the more notable for being won against these odds: more significant however is the fact that the fruits of victory were nil inasmuch as the enemy still held down the all important main couloir. The following years saw Sparta a helpless prisoner in her own territory while Argos and Corinth sank their difficulties to form one united state, a combination which, had it lasted, would have exemplified the successful realisation of the first option open to this communications area, namely the emergence of a regional power of the first rank.

The victory of Iphicrates for the Corinthians over the Spartan troops returning from Sicyon to their base at Lechaion (390 B.C.) illustrates not so much the importance of the peltasts at the time but, once again, the uselessness of approaching the Isthmus from Sicyon leaving the exposed right vulnerable to a hostile Corinth. Only the King's Peace dissolving the union in 386 B.C. rescued Sparta from the strategic impasse the union of her ancient rivals in the north-east has occasioned.[46]

Finally, the second battle of Mantinea, in 362 B.C.[47] Mantinea's isolated position well illustrates the importance of the highway, as does the Athenian plan to send troops by sea, since Argos and Tegea between them threatened to block any advance to the zone of conflict. Epaminondas' strategic supremacy showed itself in the flexibility with which he could march, now on Sparta, now on Mantinea, keeping the enemy guessing. In this situation, his victory was no surprise and is but a last example of the advantage conferred by command of the key communications in this area.

Control of the route, and with it the northeast Peloponnese, might have been the launching site for a *prostasia* of central Hellas. So it was perceived by the Corinthians and Argives of the fifth century, when, in the two decades following the Persian wars each made a separate bid in separate ways for mastery of the highway. The failure of both has obliterated the memory of their attempts, hinted at obscurely in the historical and epigraphic records of the time. The present essay seeks to reconstruct the story of a lost episode intelligible only in terms of 'l'étude des groupement humains dans leurs rapports avec le milieu géographique',[48] that is, a cultural study, superimposed on a groundwork of physical geography.

Chapter II

THE POLITICS OF THE REGION
TO 480 B.C.

The cultural background of the northeast Peloponnese

So well-established and convenient a thorough-fare not only attracted commercial traffic of the region but also, inevitably, served as the focus of political life as well: in this way arose the possibility of several and alternative political associations involving city states adjacent to the route, a true 'possibiliste' relation between society and communications. An analysis of the cultural background of the area and also of its politics forms the bulk of the present chapter, as a sequel to the geographical account in chapter one of the physical context of these politics.

The mood of archaic politics was less secular than is at times supposed. Preoccupation with some kind of timeless 'Rechtsform' too easily misses the curious mixture of emergent theory and traditional scruple characteristic of political life in the sixth century. Larsen, for example, distinguishes artificially between oaths and treaties in his account of the constitution of the Peloponnesian League, when it is clear from Herodotus 6.74 that at this epoch the oath *was* the treaty.[49] Cleomenes, trying to form an Arcadian league against Sparta, 'bound them by various oaths to follow him whithersoever he should lead, and was even desirous of taking their chief leaders with him to the city of Nonacris that he might swear them to his cause by the waters of the Styx', an episode some seventeen years later than the formation of the Peloponnesian League itself.[50]

Snodgrass'[51] study of archaic Greece underlines the central role of religion. It is cult, rather than walls or urbanization *per se* which, for him, identifies the polis; as eighth-century dedications to a patron divinity or hero are followed by the provision for a cult in the agora and ultimately by a stone temple, so the city itself comes into being *pari passu* as the distinctive creation of a distinctive *mentalité*.[52] The mythology that lies behind this development is, he argues, the dynamic of the whole era, interwoven with every other aspect: he returns frequently to the force of Greek myth as the key analytical element in his account.[53] The myth affected the present, as when Pheidon claimed the heritage of Temenus and the present affected the myth as when Agamemnon was represented as king of Argos (and not Mycenae).[54]

The importance of religion and of this particular religion had far reaching consequences, for it, more directly than any geographical obstacle, led to the fragmentation and variety characteristic of the Greek poleis. Where 'theology and dogma were wholly absent',[55] where the particular rite in the particular site was everything, it was inevitable that each community would come to manifest a unique religious and cultural profile. Pausanias was therefore right to focus on the little shrines and altars as well as the major temples: it was the sum of all these that gave to each locality its own cultural tradition, a tradition which, we may guess, was *more* marked, then, at its inception than at any later period.

Mircea Eliade's categorization of religious experience enables a differentiation between cults on a basis other than that of purely temporal sequence.[56] He concentrates on identifying as precisely as possible 'the phenomenon of the sacred in all its complexity' and at any given time or place the modality put upon 'das Heilige' by societies and, eventually, by individuals. Eliade's originality lies partly in his post-Jungian approach (he himself contributed to the Eranos Jahrbuch), partly in his denial of any opposition between what is 'natural' and what is 'sacred' — for him it is the profane which confronts the natural and the sacred both.[57]

If his observations are applied to the main areas of our region, it will be seen that three distinct and contrasting religions are present, those of Arcadia, of Argolis, and of Corinth. To anticipate, it will be seen that the Arcadian hierophanies of a non-agricultural world differ greatly from Argolic religion with its valorization of time and the unilinear historic process (genealogy, legends) and differ again from the agricultural rituals of Corinth with its articulate myths and symbols of death and rebirth. Three such different orientations, it is argued, would not easily coalesce, and since it has already been shown that at this particular epoch the content of religion in politics was still high, it follows that the likelihood of lasting association on a political basis was slight in the Archaic period, even though physical factors, that is the logic of communications, spoke strongly for such an association. In the religious culture of each area was that which would blend and that which would repel or be repelled: and at this date the latter outweighed the former.

Arcadia. Preeminent among the cults of Arcadia was the worship of Zeus Lykaios, celebrated on Mt Lykaon (Diaphorti) in Southwest Arcadia. Here the bare mountain-top precinct, encircled by a ring of unworked stones, was sacred ground, so sacred that deliberate trespass merited death as punishment. It is significant that the sanctity of the mountain-top seems to have preceded the advent of Zeus to these arts: 'Der Gott Zeus Λύκαιος heisst aber nach dem Berg, τὸ Λύκαιον ὄρος; das Epitheton ist also eine Lokalbezeichnung – die Etymologie muss von der Ortsbezeichnung ausgehen.'[58] Etymologically, in fact, the derivation from the root λυκ – light rather than λύκος – wolf is certain: to confirm the philological argument there is the ancient association of light with the area, nearby Lycosoura, for example, was the 'first city on which the sun ever shone', while the shadow-free precinct was also named Olympos by the Arcadians, and is so designated on coinage of the Arcadian League. Mt Lykaon then was a cult-place of intense sanctity and the cult of Zeus Lykaios correspondingly localized to an exceptional degree.

Zeus Lykaios was not only locally but iconographically peculiar to Arcadia. He alone carried the shepherd's crook, for example, and although the association of Zeus and the oak-tree was general throughout Greece, it had particular meaning for the Arcadians, the βαλανηφάγοι or acorn eaters, as Delphi called them: Zeus Lykaios' priest made rain with an oak branch, the chief mint of the Arcadians stamped acorns on the coins of Mantinea. Nilsson commented on the cult as a

21

whole, 'Lykaion galt gewissermassen als das Nationalheiligtum Arkadiens.' Only one place and one society could claim the cult as theirs.[59]

Next only to Zeus, the Arcadians venerated Demeter, a Demeter Nilsson distinguishes from the Eleusinian as Πότνια Θηρῶν rather than Ceres legifera: the animals that characterize the iconography of the cult he sees as theriomorphic survivals, indicative of the backwardness of Arcadian religion generally. 'In Arkadien haben sich primitive Vorstellungen zäh erhalten; es nimmt nicht wunder, unter ihnen Reste des Theriomorphismus zu finden.'[60]

The theriomorphism survived as more than a mere artistic idiosyncracy. In Thelpousa and Phigaleia the equine character of the goddess was affirmed in both legend and statuary; it was near Thelpousa that Demeter, transformed into a mare, brought forth Kore and the stallion Arion: Meyer in 'Neue Peloponnesische Wanderungen' found the probable site of this sanctuary and even the clay mould of a votive statuette of horse and rider: Thelpousan coins had Demeter's head on the obverse, a horse on the reverse. South near Phigaleia in the gorge of the Neda, was a cave sanctuary of Demeter containing the famous horse-headed statue: Demeter showed her approval of the statue by demanding a replica when the original was destroyed in fire.[61] Nor is it far from Phigaleia to Lykosoura where the marble draperies of Demeter are decorated with men wearing horses' heads.[62]

When a cult lays any stress upon one particular animal, associates the cult figure with it, identifies, for example numismatically, the community with the animal's representation, one does not have to be Lévi-Strauss to see that other animals and their communities are ipso facto being excluded. For this is the fons et origo of theriomorphism, to mark off who do and who do not belong in a given society.[63]

Thus the principal cults of Arcadia emphasized the identity of the Arcadians as a particular people in a particular area,[64] and it remains to examine the effect on Arcadian political history in the period 700—580 B.C. In passing, however, it may be noted that the image Arcadian religion enjoyed abroad was of a superstitious crudity, stories of human sacrifice, of lycanthrophy, and indeed of statues with animal heads contributing to the portrait of a race of superstitious uplanders.

22

Argos. Through much of Greek history, Argos stood apart from the other centres of Greece, a sullen enigma pursuing her own ends. The roots of this isolation are to be found in Argive culture, in the fact that her rich heritage of myth, 'the most conspicuous of the Greek pedigrees', was relatively early abused and mishandled.[65] What Murray says of Sparta, viz. that it overvalued the past and used [or abused] its mythology is at least as true of Argos; whereas the constant menace to Sparta, which explains this threat, was internal, Argos, for her part, was always under pressure from hostile neighbours. Turning myth into epic into propaganda, they debased their own spirituality. The remembrance of the heroic past became an exercise in civic pride and the confirmation of Argive superiority. To the extent that the Argives demythologized the past, they cut themselves off from the cultures of the rest of the Peloponnese.

Pausanias' impressions of the Argolid reflect this ethnocentrism. Memorials of the legendary kings who once ruled not only Argos but the whole Peloponnese were conspicuous from the frontier on: Inachus, Phoroneus, Argos himself, not to mention Temenus who held down the northeast in the early days of the Dorian conquest. The prominent part played by Argives in the epic cycles was not allowed to escape notice, from the so-called 'Rams' (Thyestes' burial place on the boundary with Mycenae) to what must have been a striking parade of statues in the heart of the city: the Seven against Thebes individually commemorated, together with the eight who subsequently captured Thebes. Argos' part in the Trojan War received scattered memorials: the graves of he warriors, the place of their oath taking, the relics of their return, as well as a temple put up to 'sharp-sighted' Athena by Diomedes and a sanctuary to Eilythuia erected by Helen after Clytemnestra's birth, which gave its name to the main gate of Argos. There are, too, Argos' own local heroes such as Cleobis and Biton, and Adrastos also, whose house Pausanias was shown and with whom local sentiment identified strongly.[66] The richness, in one sense, of Argive history and the poverty, in another sense, of a spirituality so strained and stretched to bolster national pride is visible everywhere in the itinerary, particularly if it is compared for example with the traveller's survey of Corinth and Sparta where the distinction between myth and history had not been blurred in the same way.

Allied to the emptying of the mythological past of its religious content and a suspiciously selective tradition of gods and heroes was the exclusive emphasis of Argive ceremonial. Argos was not alone in commemorating victories and victorious campaigns. Victory for victory there were more trophies in Sparta, who won more. It is more in the chauvinism of the victory celebrations that the Argive ethos appears: in the unusual and military character of the Argive games, the *Aspis* at which the prize was no wreath but a shield; and at the Nemean games, in the development of the Opheltes story as an episode from the quasinational epic of the Seven against Thebes, once the games were firmly in Argos' grip.[67] The Argive impulse to transform the sacred into the secular and political appears clearly and with it a corresponding solipsism of institutions and pageantry.

Corinth. In contrast to Argos, Archaic Corinth embodies a genuine moment in the spiritual spectrum, where the *Geistes-leben* is that of a settled agricultural people, focused on the sowing and reaping of the harvest and on the chthonic divinities that accompany this preoccupation.[68] The sanctuary of Demeter and Kore on Acrocorinth admirably illustrates this point.

The vitality of Corinth's religious life is as characteristic of the ancient city as the wealth of her trade, as proverbial, as persistent, as enticing to the contemporary Mediterranean. It is possible that this very vitality, inhibiting the transformation of myth into legend, lies at the root of a lack of historical consciousness which Malten, for one, detected in Corinthian culture. Corinth was 'sagenlos' precisely because she was so rich in myth.[69]

Excavations in the Temple Hill area of Palaio-Korinthos supply evidence of the persistence of early divinities as cult figures rather than historical personages, Medea for example, and her children, also Glauke, Hellotis, Bellerophon, and, for this argument the most significant, the syncretized deities Ino-Leucothea and their sons Melikertes-Palaimon. 'Religious traditions, apparently predating Dorian Corinth, persisted' whereas in other centers, divine figures such as these, *kourotrophoi* and *kouroi*, *paredroi* of the mother, tended to be obliterated by the Olympian pantheon, and to survive

24

as legend rather than in myth and cult. In Corinth, however, in a culture where the hierophanies were vital and significant, the old cults persisted alongside the new, limiting in a striking fashion the way in which the Olympians were worshipped. It has for example been noted with surprise that though Poseidon was the presiding god of the Isthmus and its festivals, yet the tradition continues to speak more of other, older cults of Melikertes, Theseus, Aktaion.[70] There was in fact a marked duality about the Isthmian festival, for if in classical times the games were held in honour of Poseidon, yet they were founded in honour of Palaimon, and this dual patronage — 'patronage simultané' — was at Corinth no mere formality but affected the character of the festival. The Palaimon cult stamped the games more strongly than the less marked cult of Poseidon, which was, according to Will, 'une présence diffuse et latente du dieu dans la domaine corinthien'.[71] It was the Palaimon cult that provided the protodionysiac, chthonic motifs by which observers such as Plutarch's sources and Pausanias were struck.[72]

It is argued then that Corinth's spiritual vigour is shown in the retention as cults and myths, rather than legends and history, of the older deities, and in the coherent presentation of an agrarian and mystic spirituality which inhibited the development of Olympian cults such as Poseidon's.

But this is not to say Corinthian culture was conservative or reactionary. Where a new hierophany fitted in with the essence of their religion, the Corinthians were quick to welcome — and to syncretize. Cypriot Aphrodite[73] and Adonis might have come from the east but the cult given them in Corinth was Corinth's own, neither eastern nor 'echt' 'hellenisch'. If Detienne[74] is right, the *hierodouleia* as there practised, expressed a religious movement peculiar to archaic Corinth: the old temple of Demeter and Kore (vegetation) being balanced by the new rites to Kypris.

This very vitality, however, prevented, as will be shown, the use of what traditions there were to achieve a political affiliation with the other centers. The Isthmian festival was too truly religious to be viable as the vehicle of secular politics. Its open-ended, syncretistic character was not appealing to cities with a meagre but exclusive heritage.

Thus none of our three *mentalités*, neither the Arcadian with its archaic theriomorphs and non-calendular worship, nor the Argive with its chauvinist and desacralized nationalism, nor yet the exuberant but wholly sacral and non-secular Corinthian, offered much to either of the others in the way of associative temptation.

The history of Arcadia before 480 B.C.

The accessibility of south Arcadia from Laconia involved these communities — Mantinea and Tegea, and even Orchomenus — in constant tension on the frontier. This tended to result for the rest of Arcadia in a direction of political action away from Argos and Corinth, and a negative attitude towards coalescence or alliance of any durable kind with the other hegemons of the roadway. But further, a closer inspection of the episodes of this early period reveals a total fusion of religion and politics, and in particular the isolating quality of Arcadian religion sketched out in the preliminary description.

Three episodes will be discussed: the coalition against Sparta in the mid-seventh century; the early victories of the Arcadians over Sparta in the first part of the sixth century; and the well known 'Bones of Orestes' episode in the mid-sixth century, heralding the abandonment of outright annexation as the aim of Spartan expansion.

The coalition against Sparta during the Second Messenian War. When the Messenians again took up arms against the Spartans, it was because they had heard of the defeat that Argos under Pheidon had inflicted on Sparta at the battle of Hysiae, 669 B.C. But although it was an Argive victory that touched off the revolt, nonetheless the most striking feature of the protracted and heroic struggle was its encapsulation: the ability of the Spartans to contain hostilities within a narrow corner of northeast Messenia and the inability of the Messenians and their allies to escalate the fighting in any direction. The proximity to one another of the important places in the Second Messenian War has not gone unnoticed; Forrest writes:

> There is a strong suggestion in the sources that it may have been fairly local, that whatever help may have come further afield, the

26

core of the Messenian alliance and the chief centre of conflict lay in and around northern Messenia, the area between the river Alpheios and the headwaters of the Parnisos.[75]

Moreover, the case against any widespread conflagration in the Peloponnese has been gaining ground: there is much to be said for the view that no *sustained* confrontation took place between Argos and Sparta for example (despite Hysiae) until after the submission of Tegea in the sixth century.[76] So in this instance also: of the possible distant participants, Argos and Sicyon, Argos may have left the alliance almost as soon as she joined it, if Meltas' deposition followed the division of the lands won at Hysiae and if it was the gift of these to Arcadian exiles that prompted his downfall. The participation of Sicyon is not given by Strabo but by Pausanias alone, which means the unreliable *Messeniaka* of Rhianos was the sole source for this detail. These two episodes excepted, the 'grand coalition' was indeed localized to northeast Messenia and southwest Arcadia, and the implications of the Messenian defeat confined to that area, to the zone of the actual fighting: Hira, Phigaleia, Ithome, and the Neda valley. Arcadia's preoccupation with Sparta at this date therefore diverted her attention from the problems and possibilities of the northeast Peloponnese.

The geographical factor was accompanied by a cultural isolation and the circumstances ending the second Messenian war well illustrate the still archaic nature of Arcadian politics. In spite of the scepticism with which many regard it, the story of the treachery of Aristocrates and of his violent end derives probability from the fact that it was known to Callisthenes in the fourth century.[77] A notable detail is the reaction of the Arcadians to the discovery of their leader's treason:[78]

> When this [the Spartan letter of thanks] was publicly announced, the Arcadians proceeded to stone Aristocrates with their own hands and exhorted the Messenians to do so also. The Messenians looked to Aristomenes, but he kept his eyes on the ground and wept. So the Arcadians stoned Aristocrates to death and cast him unburied beyond the boundaries.[79]

This stoning, within the actual precinct of Lycean Zeus and the ejection of his remains outside the precinct is at one with the fact that any who knowingly entered were stoned to death. Plutarch adds the detail that such a person was called 'a deer'[80]: it would seem that stoning still had much of its sacral significance for the Arcadians, whereas elsewhere it had lost it.[81]

The Battle of the Fetters. When next we find the Arcadians at war, the same two points are evident. Again Arcadian involvement is south and southwestward, spearheaded by the same cities, Tegea in principal; again, the idiosyncratic religion of the Arcadians reinforces the turning away from involvement with the northeast.

The ultimate cause of the Spartan attacks on Arcadia in the sixth century was victory in Messenia ca. 650 B.C., securing their rear and opening up a number of minor routes into the heart of Arcadia from the west. The cohesion of the Arcadians and the concerted opposition they put up against the invaders involved Sparta in a series of defeats in the first decades of the century. At Tegea, at Orchomenus, and at two other unknown places in Arcadia the Spartans were defeated and their soldiers taken prisoner. At Tegea indeed the captured Spartans were forced to put on the fetters they had brought for the Tegeates and to till the land as serfs, just as they had enslaved so many from Messenia, and afterwards, when peace had been made, these fetters were kept in the temple of Athena Alea as a reminder that the rise of Lacedaemon had not gone unchecked.[82]. Forrest supposes a confrontation between southwest Arcadia and northern Lacedaemon that was simply an extension of the second Messenian war:[83] the emphasis is wrongly put: it was this area that attracted the burden of the fighting just because it was and always had been Arcadia's continuing flashpoint.

The details of Pausanias' account, combined with the notices of the battle in Herodotus and Deinias of Argos, reveal a society in Tegea distinct from the organization of communities in less isolated regions at this date, 560 B.C. The presence of a reigning queen is unique for the period — other so-called 'queens' — such as Athens' — are priestesses.[84] The 'foundation' of the victory by the inauguration of a commemorative festival is not unusual in itself (indeed Eliade considers such 'foundations' as the mainstream of creative cult), but the all-female celebration of Ares Gynaikothoinas[85] is, again, evocative of a less integrated mode of living in the polis than other regions of the northeast Peloponnese had developed.[86]

The Bones of Orestes[87]. The two phenomena that the anti-Spartan coalition and the Battle of the Fetters displayed: a preoccupation with the southern frontier (and *pari passu* a disengagement from the northeast) and, secondly, a continuing if not increasing gap in culture between the Arcadian upland hamlets and the fast articulating cities of the Peloponnesian periphery below; these two phenomena are again apparent in the well-known episode of the bones of Orestes. The sequence of the events itself is not unclear. Sparta, deterred by a succession of fruitless campaigns against the Arcadians, Tegea in particular, opted for alliance rather than annexation as the keystone of her Peloponnesian policy, 'this sea-change in Lakonian affairs'(Cartledge), 'the Lakedaimonian government's new claim to be the true inheritor of the Achaean overlordship' (Huxley).[88] Whether there was confusion between Oresthes and Orestes, whether the Spartans created the confusion if it was not already there, whether they later hoped to repeat the Tegea coup with the discovery of the bones of Tisamenus of Elis,[89] at all events the discovery of the bones of Orestes was the key to Sparta's final success in Arcadia.

Much has been written about the ephors who planned the strategy and the evidence in Sparta for a great propaganda victory. What is more interesting is the Tegeate reaction to the fait accompli. The Achaeans in the northern Peloponnese were left unmoved by the discovery and transference to Sparta of Tisamenus' bones. The Arcadians on the other hand abadoned their century-long resistance. Demoralized by the loss of the skeleton, it was not long before they succumbed completely, concluding a treaty with Sparta and becoming from then on her staunchest ally.

The treaty of ca. 550 B.C. which spelled out the consequences of the loss of the bones was between equals:[90]

Λακεδαιμόνιοι Τεγεάταις διαλλαγέντες ἐποιήσαντο συνθήκας στήλην ἐπ' Ἀλφειῷ κοινὴν ἀνέστησαν, ἐν ᾗ μετὰ τῶν ἄλλων γέγραπται "Μεσσηνίους ἐκβαλεῖν ἐκ τῆς χώρας, καὶ μὴ ἐξεῖναι 'χρηστοὺς' ποιεῖν."

29

In spite of Jacoby's efforts to interpret χρηστοὺς ποιεῖν as 'to enfranchise', there is not sufficient reason to reject Aristotle's explanation out of hand.[91] Aristotle had said in interpretation that the pro-Spartan party in Tegea was not to be punished for its sympathies, and criticism of his interpretation has assumed that the Tegeates were at a disadvantage, the defeated party; Herodotus' account gives this view some support. However, the fact that the annexation policy was dropped by Sparta, that a treaty between equals was concluded, that there still were strong anti-Spartan elements in Tegea, shows that the Spartans were not cracking the whip militarily: instead the loss of the bones had brought a demoralized Arcadia to heel in and of itself, while the same policy had no effect at all on the more sophisticated Achaeans of the Corinthian Gulf. The cultural idiosyncracy[92] of Arcadia is clearly shown by these contrasting reactions to the same political event.

Cleomenes' Arcadian intriques[93]

The transfer of Orestes' bones to Sparta brought peace to Arcadia for a time at least. Psychological warfare had achieved what a century of Spartan hoplites had failed to secure. But the preoccupation of the Arcadians with their southern border and their simplistic and superstitious *Weltanschauung* continued, as is shown by the next major episode in their history: Cleomenes' intrigues.

It is important first to establish the nature of Spartan-Arcadian relations after the Orestes episode. What was the nature of Sparta's ascendancy? Did it rest on separate treaties sworn with separate states? Was the pillar which Aristotle saw, which embodied the terms of the Spartan-Tegeate peace, the first of a series of such agreements? What was involved for either side? Mutual defence only, or, in addition, participation in the more adventurist wars of either party, or neither of these things? This last is not impossible: the treaty could have confined itself to territorial definitions and the treatment of friends and fugitives in each other's domains.

It is, however, assumed by many — notably Busolt–Swoboda — that first Tegea and then the other Arcadian states joined a Spartan-led alliance and were thereafter committed to sending contingents on Spartan-led expeditions.

Sicherlich wurden sie in erster Linie zur Bundesgenossenschaft und Heeresfolge verpflichtet. Darnach müssen sich ihnen auch die übrigen Arkaden unterordnen soweit sie es nicht bereits getan hatten.[94]

Then, according to the general understanding, these separate treaties were replaced in 506 or 505 by the calling of a constitutional convention and the drafting of a constitution for all the allies, which defined their rights and obligations in a confederation with its own regularly meeting assembly. This is Larsen's construction, whose approach to archaic politics was criticized briefly at the start of this chapter, while he himself expresses clearly the doubts students of Greek history will have as to his conventions and constitutions, though he seems to feel that to have expressed these doubts is to have exorcised them.[95] The only 'contemporary' parallel, a quarter of a century later, the organization of the Delian League, still gives off an air of unsophisticated personalities and antiquated ceremonial.[96] Later parallels whether from Andocides' speeches, from Xenophon's Hellenica, or even Diodorus, are obviously anachronistic as evidence for the diplomatic style of 506 B.C.

If then the existence of a diplomatic apparatus of individual treaties and collective pacts is rejected, what kind of bonds are we to suppose Sparta employed to control her former enemies? How was Arcadia held down from 560 to 495 B.C.?

An answer has been suggested by Forrest.[97] Discussing the passage of the law at Sparta which enacted that in future both kings would not appear on the field of battle together, he argues that 'If the original treaties had contained a promise to follow wherever not the Spartans but *the kings* [my italics] might lead, to keep one king at home would automatically free the ally from his obligations.' Aegina, for one, Forrest points out, refused to take advantage of the casuist's loophole. The inference is that the tie between Sparta and her allies was personal, king to king, ruler to ruler, based on oaths of allegiance which involved all manner of penalties on the man who was forsworn. Defiance was always a possibility and the bond was coterminous with the life of the local ruler and no stronger than his authority.

It was this kind of relationship that Cleomenes drew on when in 490 he attempted to raise Arcadia against Sparta, making the chieftains again swear allegiance to him at the waters of Styx as we have already noted. It was on the latent independence of these communities that Hegesistratos relied when he fled to Tegea, 'Tegea being at that time at variance with Sparta.'[98] This individualist interpretation of the political bond would also explain why it was on their generals that the Mantineans took revenge for the lateness of their own contingent at Plataea, yet the Spartans thought themselves justified in denying the whole city-state mention on the serpent column.[99] The continued vigour of all the Arcadian communities: Parrhasia, Maenalus, Cleitor, Heraea, not to mention Tegea and Mantinea themselves, can only be explained by an interpretation of the Peloponnesian League from 560 to 460 B.C. that rejects formal, impersonal constitutional machinery in favour of intermittent, unreliable bonds of allegiance between princes. Sparta is again using the peculiarities of the Arcadians against them, and again Arcadia's cultural archaism is found reinforcing her preoccupation with the south, pulling her away from closer ties with east and northeast.

The history of Argos before 480 B.C.

It may be true, as Snodgrass observes, that Argos was but one among many 'conquest-states', sharing with them the characteristics of 'deep-rooted and lasting aristocratic tendencies' and 'leaning towards militarism too'. Tomlinson, however, sees in the pattern of Argive development a further, distinctive feature:

> It is possible to detect a certain cynicism in the manipulation of festivals and taboos for a completely non religious political purpose.[100]

In other words the conservative exclusive ethos had hardened, in Argos, into a perceptible policy of aggrandisement.

Pheidon. Andrewes, among the earliest to interpret Pheidon of Argos as a forerunner of the tyrants and exponent of the new art of hoplite democracy, was also aware that the Argive use of the slogan 'the heritage of Temenus' (Λῆξις Τημένου)

32

played a large part in the campaign to recover the northeast Peloponnese which Pheidon undertook in the middle of the seventh century.[101] Political claims based on the return of the Heraclidae were not uncommon, Tegea for example arguing with more logic than tact that she deserved the left wing at Plataea because of her champion's defeat of Hyllos and her own subsequent defeat of Sparta.[102] The content of Pheidon's claim, however, deserves closer analysis as it indicates the exclusivism of the Argive ethos and the aggrandisement which formed their foreign policy. For after all who but the Argives was interested in restoring Temenus' heritage? As Burns observes, the non-Dorian people would be as little attracted as the non-Temenid Dorian stock to such a rallying-cry.[103] No coalition or alliance would crystallize about so irredentist a platform: predictably none of the neighboring states displayed the least enthusiasm. Corinth seems to have made a point of rejecting the Aeginetan standard Pheidon proposed for the area, and whether this happened in Pheidon's lifetime or more probably later, it shows that the result of Pheidon's policy was to repel, not to attract, the other communities of the region.[104] Pheidon's only allies were the Pisatans, who, whoever they were, did not form part of Temenus' portion of the Peloponnese. Epidaurus, Hermione, Troezen, Cleonae, Nemea, Phlius, not to mention Sicyon, all involved in Argos' claim, did their best to stay out of Pheidon's adventures.

Militarism was the natural accompaniment of this racial exclusiveness. At Hysiae, Pheidon and his hoplites defeated the army of Lacedaemon, a momentous event which at once set Messenia alight with rebellion.[105] Andrewes points out that at this period the Argives, not the Spartans, were the military power par excellence and in support he adduces the curious oracle contrasting 'the linen-corsleted Argives, the goads of war' with the worthless Megarians, the horse-proud Thessalians, and the Spartans endowed with fair women.[106] The hoplites at Hysiae and their new tactics were the foundation of Pheidon's brief ascendancy. It is still possible that in the pyramidal graves of the Argolid at Cenchreae we have, as Pausanias says, the city's recognition of their valour.[107]

After Hysiae, Pheidon tried to supplement military victory with diplomatic initiative, namely the presidency and reorganization of the Olympic Games. The rise of the Crown Games in the century 660—560 B.C. was seen by Bury as the expression of a growing panhellenism alongside the intensifying local loyalties of the city-states.[108] Yet this contrast is spurious, anachronistic; for in fact the Crown Games arose and continued throughout the Archaic Period as the primary, almost the only counters in the bid any sizable state might make for regional hegemony. It will be seen below that Argos could not maintain control over the Eleans and their festival: she then turned closer home for a festival to patronize and taking up the Nemean festival made it another vehicle for Argive nationalism.

Sixth century Argos: the Kulturkampf. It was argued earlier that Corinth overtly repulsed Argos' seventh century overtures, whether cultural (the Aeginetan standard) or political (if Pheidon did in fact die in a struggle with Corinth itself). In the next century Sicyon's refusal to adhere to any reformed Temenid inheritance was even more forthright. For this is the meaning of Cleisthenes' expulsion of the hero Adrastus, his banning of Homeric recitations (too much praise of Argos), and his institution of the Theban Melanippus as hero in the Argive Adrastus' place.[109]

It is interesting to note that Adrastus' bones were to be flung physically beyond Sicyonian territory.[110] This was contemporary with Lichas' appropriation of the bones of Orestes from Tegea and shows that this was still the age of bones, shrines, and games as the material of interstate relations.

Cleisthenes himself turned to the Delphic festival for prestige and aggrandisement. Possibly it was in conscious imitation of Pheidon that he took part in the First Sacred War and in 582 B.C. instituted the Pythian Games, underlining their associations with Sicyon by establishing other, local, Pythia. It will not have been ironic that these local Pythia were later on held in honour of Adrastus: it simply indicates that at the time when this later association was made, the councillors in the bouleuterion of Sicyon were in favour of closer ties with Argos.[111]

This interpretation of Cleisthenes' policies as the explicit reply to unsuccessful and maladroit Argive tentatives towards association helps to explain why, when Sparta suppressed the

Sicyonian tyranny in the 550's, the anti-Argive gestures were not at once repealed, and when, sixty years later, the old Dorian tribal names returned, the fourth, non-Dorian tribe, was given the honourable name of Aigialeis after the mythical founder of the city. Sparta had no interest in promoting pro-Argive attitudes or encouraging the creation of a rival zone in the region.[112]

For it was at this date that an armed struggle between Argos and Sparta took place, establishing the preëminence of Sparta for the remainder of the century. After Pheidon, Argos could still assert herself. Though unable to control the Olympian Games, she reacted to Cleisthenes' Pythian festival with the presidency of the Nemean festival, whose foundation in the Olympiad 572—568 B.C. will be dealt with in greater detail in Chapter 3. It is sufficient to insist here that whatever the exact division of honours at the early Nemean Games between Argos and Cleonae, the relationship was that of Argive suzerainty over a client state. Argive protection of and participation in the Nemean games was such as to give the instant association of Argos with the games that Pindar and Bacchylides evoke;[113] and was also, as suggested earlier, such as to result in their being more nationalistically Argive than other festivals were local in identification.[114]

Argos also dominated a local amphictiony (as Cleisthenes did in Crisa) and again, whatever the exact constitutional relationship between Argos and the other states in the amphictiony, it is clear that Argos meant the league to be an instrument for the furtherance of Argive interests and the establishment of a hegemony, part cultural, part military.

> Die argeiische Konföderation hatte demnach zweifellos einen religiösen Charakter, doch darf man dabei nicht die politische Seite derselben ganz in den Hintergrund stellen.[115]

We may note that the choice of Apollo Pythaeus over Hera as patron would once again alienate the sympathies of a number of Argos' natural allies, namely the men of Mycenae and Tiryns and all the remnant of the Achaian Argolid, for Apollo Pythaeus was an exclusively Dorian divinity.[116] Argive propaganda excluded many and attracted none.

The amphictiony indeed seems to have been even less convincing politically than Pheidon's restored Temenid heritage of the previous century. Its appearance in history is invariably in connection with a break of its rules and on one significant occasion when it arranged the so-called Battle of Champions in Thyreatis, the conventions were so wholly maladroit that the archaic contest of champions gave way before long to an all out mêlée of rival armies.[117] For all that the Argives were defeated, however, it is a mistake to indentify the loss of the Thyreatis with the finish of Argos as a Peloponnesian rather than a purely Argolic power. Sparta's alliances with Argive satellites such as Hermione and Troezen cannot be dated to this early period. It is truer to say that Argos left the sixth century as she had begun it, a strong community but lacking any attraction for the neighbouring states.

Fifth century Argos: Cleomenes. It was Cleomenes who was to change this situation permanently at Sepeia. Allowing for exaggeration, the death of 6,000 Argives was a calamity without precedent for Argos — or for Greece.[118] When in 426 the Ambraciots lost over 1,000 men, Thucydides cannot bring himself to name the exact total, but remarks that this was the worst disaster to befall any one city in the war. Argos was a larger state than the Ambraciot nation, but nonetheless if we consider the contingents at Plataia in 479: 5,000 Spartans, 5,000 Corinthians, 8,000 Athenians, and also the Athenian strength 60 years later in 431 B.C., when the hoplite force was 13,000, it can be seen how immense a calamity the loss of 6,000 hoplites will have been.[119] Lenschau, arguing for the earlier date for Sepeia, explains the implication of this loss in manpower for the front line of 40 years on, and compares this situation with the Athenian refusal to support Agesilaus in 396 B.C. on account of a manpower shortage, for which the Athenians held the plague of 34 years earlier responsible. Even if we disagree with Lenschau's earlier date, his remarks about the extent to which Argos' future was crippled by Sepeia still hold: indeed, they seemed echoed by the words of the Argive envoys to the Greeks in 480 B.C. whose price for assistance against the Mede was a thirty years' truce with Sparta 'to give time for their children to grow to man's estate'[120] After Sepeia for forty years the Argives had to repress as far as possible their natural inclination to respond to challenge or opportunity with military force, though the other component of their culture, chauvinism, remained undimmed as the request for joint command of the Greek army with Sparta in 480 showed.

Fifth century Argos. It has been argued that after Sepeia Argos was forced, through loss of manpower, to extend the citizenship to many of the surrounding communities (polismata) which had till then been dependencies.[121] The argument (not unreasonably) takes perioikoi in Aristotle[122] and Plutarch[123] to mean, as in Lacedaemon, inhabitants of local hamlets and the process is seen as, so to speak, a shotgun synoecism, with Argos displaying the capacity, however reluctant, to assimilate her neighbours as full citizens.

Lotze, however, in *Chiron* I[124] has demolished this reconstruction: basing himself on a rigorous examination of Aristotle's argument in POL 1302B33 — 1303A13, he can show that the people involved must be *within* the citizen body already for Aristotle's line of thought to make sense: he suggests that those who would be most likely to assume control of the affairs (property) of the fallen would be neither non-citizens nor literal *douloi* — rather, he supposes persons in a hektemor or cliens-like situation to be the ones to take over (and thus effect that disproportionate growth of one sector rather than another that in Aristotle's view led to the μεταβολαὶ πολιτειῶν[125]).

The catastrophe at Sepeia, therefore, did not cause the Argives to discard their traditional stance: such 'synoecism' as there was at Argos[126] in the fifth century was compulsory and might more properly be termed annexation.

Moreover, the sixth century Calaurian amphictiony, whether strictly an amphictiony or not, which bound Argos and the perioikic townships, was still operative after Sepeia, since it legitimated Argive fines on Sicyon and Aegina for aid to Cleomenes.[127] There is no reason to suppose the Argives at this crisis in their history abandoned the traditional amphictiony of Apollo Pythaeus for any kind of synoecism along Athenian lines.

Thus an interpretation of post-Sepeia Argos as in liberal or assimilative mood is quite unjustified. Weakened but unenlightened, the Argives, as the next episode shows, adhered to their traditional ethnocentrism.

The Medism of Argos. The phenomenon of Argive Medism has attracted little attention except as in the context of the Peace of Callias. But in fact it is stranger even than the aberration of an individual such as the Spartan Pausanias, that a large Greek city state, strategically immune (unlike for example Delphi) should have embraced the Great King's cause, and without much sign of reluctance. It is not enough to exclaim 'Realpolitik!' and argue that Argos was bidding for hegemony of the Peloponnese as Persia's agent. It must be further asked how such policy was possible in a city which claimed to have inherited the leadership of the Greek mainland from Agamemnon, a Dorian community surrounded by neighbouring Dorian communities. These all seem to have felt strongly enough their obligation to fight for Hellas against the barbarian: Mycenae and Tiryns, not to mention Troezen and Epidaurus, Sicyon, Phlius, all were lined up against Mardonius at Plataea.[128] Only the exclusivism previously discussed, which grew out of the perversion of a common mythology, allowed the Argives to listen to Xerxes' arguments: that curious passage where Herodotus implicitly admits the Medism of Argos also shows what reasoning the Persians thought would attract the Argives — the appeal to a purely Argive version of ancient Greek mythology, according to which the Persians were descendants of the old rulers of Argos, a skilful awakening of the exaggerated pride in 'stock and lineage'.[129] As usual, the policy Argos adopted was the policy least likely to make her the nucleus of a coalition of northeast Peloponnesian states.

ἐχϑρὲ περικτιόνεσσι, φίλ᾽ ἀϑανάτοισι ϑεοῖσι, εἴσω τὸν προβόλαιον
ἔχων πεφυλαγμένος ἦσο καὶ κεφαλὴν πεφύλαξο. κάρη δὲ τὸ σῶμα
σαώσει.[130]

Hated of all thy neighbours, beloved of the blessed Immortals,
Sit thou still, with thy lance drawn inward, patiently watching;
Wearily guard thine head, and the head will take care of the body.

The history of Corinth before 480 B.C.

The pre-Cypselid era. Like Argos and Arcadia, Corinth also manifested a unique religious and cultural profile, of which the salient characteristics were a vitality and vigour which permitted genuine religious development to go on *continuously*. Corinth's rulers tried and failed to harness myth and ritual to their own goals. The *obverse* of this phenomenon, the integrity of the Corinthian religious experience, was the opportunity at once afforded in Corinth perhaps first of all for genuinely secular politics, at home and abroad.

Without adducing this factor of vitality, Corinth's archaic preëminence in iconography must be puzzling. Will notes that Corinth adopted the orientalizing style before Thera, 'si choquant que ce puisse paraître à première vue...une chose est de constater le fait, une autre de l'expliquer', particularly since Corinth was by no means the leader in trade with the East before 650 and her earliest commercial enterprises took her west, not east. But it was Corinth whose orientalizing art was the first to exhibit 'une réelle conscience de ses possibilités décoratives et d'une cohésion interne' and who were spiritually more ready ('plus ouverts') to accept these sympathetic trends.[131]

Corinth could stylize without deadening the exotica and erotica of the east because these motifs were allowed to permeate her own cults: the lions, twin-headed, the mermen, the gorgons, the griffins could be integrated by the Corinthian painters because, as Corinthians, they were intrigued by and would later accept the religion beyond the iconography. The success of proto-Corinthian ceramic is only part of a movement that brought ex-voto scarabs in unprecedented number to Perachora and inspired craftsmen to manufacture Astarte plaques that are clearly images of the Phoenician moon-goddess.[132]

Treatment of legend. The contrast of Corinth and Argos appears nowhere so clearly as in the development of their respective genealogies and legendary *gesta* of the city's heroes. To set against the Pelopids, the rollcall from Pelops to Orestes, the Corinthians could produce only the shakiest ancestry, 'un remplissage chronologique'[133] at worst, a heterogenous assembly of cult figures at best.

An attempt seems to have been made towards the close of the eighth century by Eumelus of Corinth to erect, for his city and for the ruling oligarchy of which he was a member, a pedigree as impressive and extended as Argos' own. Possibly, since the differing styles of the extant fragments make a single late-eighth-century date difficult, we have not so much the work of one poet as of a collective epic tradition spreading over a century ca. 750–650.[134] It is to this effort that we owe the two dynasties, five generations apiece, which run from Aietes the father of Medea to that Hyanthidas, in whose days the Dorians came to Corinth. It may well be that the *Korinthiaka* embodies the first systematic attempt to falsify history,[135] but more interesting still is the feebleness of this attempt. The artificiality of the pre-Sisyphid line's prolongation, the obvious derivation of the hero Bounos from the cult of Hera Bounaia, the bankruptcy of imagination that produced 'Sikyon' and 'Korinthos' as sons of the fourth king 'Marathon' — this incompetently prefabricated prehistory never commanded much attention.[136]

In the entire construction, two names stand out, Medea from the Aletid dynasty and Bellerophon from the Lykian branch of the Sisyphid. What both have in common is a flourishing cult and a spurious association with the cults and myths of alien shores: Thessaly, Colchis (Medea), Lydia, Caria (Bellerophon). These two divinities, viz. Medea, ancient fertility goddess eclipsed by Hera, and Bellerophon, anthropomorphic hypostasis of the horse god, pursued their own paths as the object of continuing interest and devotion from the Corinthians.[137] But the elaborate scaffolding of dates and descents into which Eumelus tried to insert these divinities failed, possibly from the first, to win interest, let alone credence. Where Argos forced myth into time-serving legend, Corinth seems to have avoided the localisation that would have turned her myths into the heritage of a single polis: thereby she preserved their integrity but forfeited, it may be, any potential anchorage-in-legend for such association as she wished to enter into with neighbouring states.[138]

Cypselid Corinth. Towards the end of the tyranny, Periander organized the Isthmian Games on a permanent basis,[139] but when he attempted to make political capital out of cult ceremony he was no more successful than the Bacchiads. A fuller account of the Isthmian Games will be given in Chapter 3: here it suffices to point out the extent to which myth and cult dominated the secular element. In various sections supra, Pheidon's presidency of the Olympic Games, Cleisthenes of Sicyon's foundation of local Pythian Games, and the Argive foundation of the Nemean festival have been interpreted as genuine political phenomena of an age where shrines, bones, and games were the recognized media of politics. In time, Periander's inauguration of the Isthmian festival falls between Cleisthenes' Pythia and the Argive Nemeans.[140]

It will be argued later that the Crown Games (Olympics, Pythians, Nemeans, Isthmians) were a new cult form — the cult of the agonistic hero — that grew during the seventh century and was systematized in the early decade of the sixth century B.C. At the Isthmus, Periander's systematization of the *Kultakt* involved the displacement of the original agon hero, Theseus, in favour of Melikertes, renamed 'Palaimon'. Melikertes, the dying child (a vegetation spirit), became the hero of the new rite; and associated with him as secondary hero was the Aletid Sisyphus, forming a parallel to the Heracles—Pelops pair at Olympia.[141]

In the event, however, Theseus did not withdraw so easily — the myth of his struggle with Sinis the Pine-bender and the association of this victory with the origin of the Isthmians lived on. Nor did the dying child shed his mystic agrarian character on becoming the agon hero — Plutarch says the ceremonies associated with Melikertes were secret and nocturnal and were more like a mystery ritual than a public celebration. This quality of τελέτη was never lost; rather the fertility cult tended to overshadow the agonistic, giving the Isthmian ceremonial its distinctive atmosphere.

> Those that were there before observed, dedicated to Melicerta, were performed privately in the night, and had the form rather of a religious rite than of an open spectacle or public feast.
> Plutarch, *Theseus*, tr. Dryden[142]

In the failure of Periander's manipulation of myth to give the cult ceremony a more national Aletid quality, we can see both the incorruptibility of Corinthian religion and its incompatibility with the cultures of Argos and Arcadia, as basis for a coalition of city states.

Introduction of Cyprian Aphrodite. Indeed the tyrants themselves were in general as interested in and receptive of new religions and divinities from abroad as their subjects. 'Sodann scheint Periandros im Gegensatz zu den altdorischen

41

Gottesdiensten die neuaufkommenden volkstümlichen Kulte gepflegt zu haben.'[143] This attitude he shared with his father Cypselus, for it was in the latter's reign that the first stonework in the precinct ('Tavern') of Aphrodite belongs, a precinct to have a long and prosperous history on the site: to Cypselus' period also is dated the earliest votive plaque to Cyprian Aphrodite in the Corinthia (Perachora).[144]

Periander himself built a temple to Aphrodite in the port of Lechaion and though Aphrodite Melainis was also then worshipped at Corinth, in view of its date and site it is more probably Aphrodite Kypria to whom Periander's new temple was dedicated.[145] On Acrocorinth stood Cyprian Aphrodite's most famous temple in Greece: the earliest building was begun under the tyranny, and though it is not certain that this earlier temple was Aphrodite's, later the site was hers.[146] It had been conjectured that it was Periander who began the *hierodouleia*, temple prostitution, practised in the temple on Acrocorinth;[147] the vestimentary holocaust to Hera, whose rites at Corinth were said to be identical with Aphrodite's may be susceptible of an explanation along these lines.[148] The obvious reason for connecting the tyranny with the introduction of Aphrodite in her particularly Cyprian form, androgynous, ἀναδυομένη, and served by temple prostitutes lies in the development and expansion of trade under the Cypselids, whereby contact with Cyprus would be increased.[149] But another, better, analysis would explain the development not merely as an index of commercial expansion but as evidence for the ongoing receptivity of the Corinthians to sympathetic cultural phenomena. To the extent, moreover, that this exotic cult was established, to that extent Corinth's neighbours in the northeast Peloponnese and in the Arcadian southern highlands were going to be reluctant to join Corinth in any lasting sociopolitical coalition.

It would be irrelevant to continue this account of Corinth's receptivity to alien moeurs, nor is the evidence as striking as in these centuries of pervasive orientalizing; but the early centuries of our era, to judge by the Apostle Paul and the writing of Apuleius and Aristides, saw a parallel floraison. Even in the absence of widespread cultural changes the trend recurs: for the immediate post-tyrannic period alone, the worship of Cybele may be adduced in support of the contention that Corinth was ever open to change in religious matters.[150]

Religious vitality, secular vitality. Increasing interest is being shown in Corinth's post-Cypselid constitution and in the suggestion that it was here that Cleisthenes found the model and inspiration for the Athenian democracy of 508/7 B.C.[151] The sources are few and anything but lucid. Suidas, commenting on πάντα ὀκτώ (everything by eights) writes

οἱ δὲ ὅτι 'Αλήτης κατὰ χρησμὸν τοὺς Κορινθίους συνοικίζων, ὀκτὼ φυλὰς ἐποίησε τοὺς πολίτας καὶ ὀκτὼ μέρη τὴν πόλιν.

Others say that Aletes when he founded Corinth in accordance with an oracle, divided the citizens into 8 tribes and the city into 8 parts.[152]

Busolt comments: Wahrscheinlich hängt sie mit der Reorganisation der Verfassung nach dem Sturze der Tyrannis zusammen.[153] First of all the suggestion of a systematic use of the numeral 8 is interesting (like Cleisthenes' 10). Second, a regional division, a tribal system based on locality, is the most natural inference. This, moreover, seems (almost) confirmed by the discovery of 4 tribal rubrics none of which can be the old Dorian tribes and which are plausibly filled out to denote areas – *Le*chaion, *Si*dous (Dow): perhaps *Sy*bota, perhaps even *Kyn*okephalaion.[154] Thus new tribes and based on locality seem likely enough. Whether Stroud's suggested trittys subdivision is correct cannot yet be told. A fiscal or military subdivision of the tribe now seems more likely.[155] Even without the trittys, though, we have sweeping reconstruction on a secular basis, the first of its kind.

Nicholas of Damascus adds further details about the operation of the post Cypselid constitution. Unfortunately they are obscure in the extreme.[156]

αὐτὸς (ὁ δῆμος) δὲ παραχρῆμα † ἐστρατεύσατο (Mue: ἐπραγματεύσατο) πολιτείαν τοιάνδε· μίαν μὲν ὀκτάδα προβούλων ἐποίησεν, ἐκ δὲ τῶν βουλὴν κατέλεξεν ἀνδρῶν Θ.

The people forthwith enacted the following constitution. They created one octad of probouloi and from the rest chose a boulé of 9 men.

Will's suggestion that the council was 80 strong, composed of one octad of probouloi (leading magistrates) and nine more members *from each tribe* (72) is very attractive. One might note (a) that the demos is credited with achieving this system and (b) that the key number 8 is just as prominent in this passage as in Suidas. Why these '8's in the boulé? Could they be like the Athenian prytaneis, the effective government (in oligarchic Corinth) for an eighth of the year? It would seem therefore that dramatic and original constitutional experiment followed the tyranny and it may actually be the success (*eunomia*[157]) of these reforms that insulated Corinth from the logographoi of the next centuries.[158]

This secularity would be the natural accompaniment of Corinth's lively and authentic religiosity. The sacred remained fresh, spontaneous, uncontaminated by being involved in the secularizing process. Alongside it, there naturally would arise the profane, the reasonable, and logically constructed government that made no use of bones, shrines, festivals, genealogies and legends. Yet Corinth's secular revolution will have appeared alarmingly avant-garde and radical her neighbours.

External politics. The same secularity informed Corinth's external policies. Sparta's system of alliances did not recover from the admission of Corinth to their number. Two crises followed in quick succession the entry of Corinth into the Peloponnesian League by which is meant not the joint expedition to Samos in 524, but the participation in the general rally of Sparta's allies for Cleomenes' third expedition against Athens (506 B.C.) and subsequently for the abortive campaign to reinstate Hippias. It is no coincidence that on both occasions it was the Corinthians who were responsible for the foundering of Sparta's plans. The first time they brought about the end of the chieftain system. Under this system the Spartans could lead out a Peloponnesian army headed by two commanders-in-chief with equal power on an expedition whose object was kept secret. On the second occasion, not long after, whatever the truth about Sosikles' speech, the residual datum would seem to be outspoken opposition by an ally for the first time, sufficiently effective to block Sparta's intentions. It will then have been Corinth's adherence to the company of Peloponnesian allies that brought the first element of a rational and co-operative approach to decision making, a process that gradually

44

developed to the not unsophisticated workings of the League as revealed in Thucydides.

Conclusion

This protracted argument has sought to show to what extent the possibilities for association offered by the arterial highway of the northeast Peloponnese had been realised by 480 B.C. It has been argued that the factor determining whether or not groups and leagues or looser ententes were formed was naturally the political, and that at this stage the material of politics, its substance not just its modus, were the phenomena of cult and religion. More speculatively, it has been argued that the cultures of three main zones, if they did nor preclude, at least made improbable the formation of a lasting union, so disparate were the modalities of their religions. A brief historical survey has shown that events bear out the a priori contention that the zones were unlikely to harmonize.

In conlcusion, a caveat should be entered about the generalizations on which these broad judgements are based. Inspection of even such evidence as we have will produce several exceptions and irregularities in the pattern: for example the ivory seals in the Argive Heraion are not less oriental in inspiration than those in the Heraia at Perachora at the same date;[159] again, as is well known, when the tyranny fell at Corinth, the bones of Periander and his family were disinterred and physically flung beyond the frontiers of Corinthian territory.[160] It is a question, however, in these generalizations, of weight of evidence one way or another, not of a few negative examples, and the cohesion of the record under the interpretation suggested goes some way, it is hoped, to counterbalance evidence that militates against it.

Chapter III

STUDY OF A POLITICO-CULTURAL PHENOMENON CHARACTERISTIC OF THE ARCHAIC PERIOD: THE CROWN GAMES

Introduction

The actualization of the possibilities for union of the city states of the northeast Peloponnese (possibilities delineated by the highway from Tegea to Corinth) was determined in the archaic period, as the previous chapter has explained, by political factors expressed in and undifferentiated from the cultural, specifically the religious, context of the period. Outside the region, in Corinth, at Athens in particular under Cleisthenes, secular politics slowly began to emancipate itself from the *Geistesleben* of its surroundings and establish its autonomy, so that once the archaic era ends, the political activities of the Greeks, their electoral wards, their assemblies, canvassing, rhetoric, ballots, qualifications for office, resemble increasingly what we now mean by political activity. There was, not surprisingly, a transitional era in which the old determinants occur, but less often, and the new more frequently. The present study suggests that the years 480—460 are part of this transitional era and lie towards its inception, so that the old elements of archaic politics of the bones-and-games variety still balance the new, autonomous, profane politics of democracies, oligarchies, radicalisms, and radically reconstructed politeiai. The two are interwined for much of the fifth century — Cleisthenes the reformer is also Cleisthenes inaugurator of the cult of the new

46

tribal heroes: Alcibiades who profaned the Mysteries marked his political return by their celebration. In the present chapter, it is one of the continuing traditional determinants that is examined.

A traditional determinant: the Panhellenic Games

The archaic period offers many examples of the amalgamation of cults with political life: belief in the vertu of relics (Orestes), incrimination of inanimate objects (Aristocrates), foundation of military victories (Choira), but it is the political function of the main athletic contests, the Panhellenic Games, which best illustrates the essence of this amalgam.

It is not only historicist but false to suppose that there was a golden age of Greek athletics in the sixth or fifth centuries before the twin evils of professionalism and the entertainments business corrupted the innocence of Hellenic sport. It would be truer to say that before professionalism and the entertainments business there was no sport, and that athletics, like politics, gradually differentiated itself during the fifth century out of a sociocultural conglomerate that was mainly what we should call religious in character and Eliade, sacred. Sport and politics belong to the profane world and neither Plato nor Thomas Arnold can put them back in the sacred.

English writers on Greek athletics such as Gardiner and Harris[161] are crippled by their conviction that athletic competitions are spontaneous and self-evidently agreeable. For this assumption makes enquiry into the origins, or discussion of the character, of the games superfluous: all that is required is an explanation of the religious aspect of the occasion. The Greeks, it is said, with their strong anthropomorphic conception of divinity assumed that the gods enjoyed displays of athletic prowess as much as they themselves did;[162] alternatively, what in contemporary contests is ascribed to luck, the Greeks found it more interesting to describe as the intervention of personal deities.[163] As for the origins of the games and their ascription so often to a hero of Greek mythology, this is said to be mere custom, with parallels at all ages.[164]

No wonder then that so much in a Greek athletic festival

47

strikes these historians as strange, for if the Panhellenic Games were simply a modern fixture plus some uncommon ceremony, it must be surprising, for example, that the program of events was so conservative, continuing unaltered for 913 years;[165] that *all* narratives of the games are in the heroic mode, devoid of fact and technicality; that so little time was spent on games, so much on ceremony; that the motif of cult outweighed the sporting interest for the spectators. Equally surprising are the inequality of the καμπτήρ, and the retention of the hoplite race, not to mention the *hippios*.[166]

What then were the Panhellenic Games? It has been argued that in the archaic age politics was religion and religion politics: so too, in the same period, sport including athletics was a part of religion, and religion part of sport, and the juxtaposition only seems incongruous because the vocabulary of physical exercise has become technical and empty. What sort of religion, then, expressed itself in these contests?

Those (such as Meuli[167]) who have recognised a tie between archaic athletic festivals and archaic religion have found its explanation in the practice of funerary games and only differ thereafter in their analyses of the intent behind this ritual:[168] was it ancestor worship, expressed in regular commemoration[169] or re-enacted reconciliation of the defunct by contests originally to the death?[170]

Leichenspiele there may well have been on both sides of the Dark Ages (Vermeule[171]) but we have little — other than the pedantry of Alexandrian scholiasts[172] — to support the theory that it is here that we are to seek the original impetus of the ἀγῶνες στεφανῖται. These "games" are, rather, a specifically archaic development, aligned to a specifically archaic religious ethos, namely, the cult of the hero, which, while not inspired, as Coldstream[173] suggests, by contemporary Homeric poems, constituted, as he and Murray[174] insist, a new and not a revived phenomenon. The connection with the cult of a particular hero might, arguably, have been funerary but this is unlikely. True funerary rituals involve *drōmena* of mutilation, of frenetic grief (Attis, Adonis) and these, Burkert[175] suggests, may express an inversion of the strive-succeed motif of many myths: may express frustration and failure, and emphasize not immortality, but death.

The spirit of the games is quite other. What is here expressed

48

by the athletic participant is, I suggest, the effort to attain by victory to the same immortality as that of the hero. Robert Jay Lifton, in *Revolutionary Immortality*[176] gives a clear account of the concept of the hero's symbolic immortality, highly relevant in his view, to the crisis of personal and historical continuity and ensuring both the immortality of the hero and the participation of the devotee in the same.[177]

For it is certainly the figure of the hero who informs psychologically the whole ambience of the sixth century games: the eternal survivor, he who is not to grow old.[178] By symbolic participation in his struggles, his *athla* and the *ponoi* that are behind him, ordinary men may join in the experience of immortality:

> Peace now and forever from his mighty struggles, with ease his prize in the halls of heaven and with radiant youth evermore his consort.[179]

This is the real inspiration in the archaic age for the sacred contests. Wilamowitz, as always, put it eloquently in his edition of Euripides' *Herakles*: Mensch gewesen, Gott geworden; Mühen erduldet, Himmel erworben.

The approach here adopted is, again in Lifton's phrase, psychohistorical, which itself requires elucidation. He defines it as

> a general perspective within which to comprehend both psychological motives and historical context — that is, a psychological framework. I propose such a framework because I believe it can reveal much about motivation behind and relationship between seemingly unfathomable and disputed events.[180]

Lifton is writing about the excess and despair of a modern revolution, but as he predicts, his analysis has relevance to other similar occasions remote in space and time.[181] Symbolic immortality, he argues, is the quest of all men collectively and individually, each man's inner perception of his involvement in the historical process. This urge a man may express biologically by having children; theologically by academic arguments as to man's nature and purpose; artistically; sensuously; and, for Lifton the key phenomenon, experientially, experiential transcendence — so intense that, at least temporarily, it eliminates time and death...such that it can approach that of religious mystics.[182] In Lifton's view it is the crisis of the hero's approaching end that generates social revolution, which he interpreted as an experiential exercise in quest of symbolic immortality.

It is argued here that the rise of the panhellenic games, the archaic games before they became secular sports, with their motifs of *ponos* (effort) and *charma* (joy), is to be interpreted in similar terms. There was first and historically a revolution brought about by the collapse of the Dark Age *oikos* and the static hierarchical world it had engendered. Colonies, coinage, hoplite armour, hoplite tactics, trade, technical advance — pressures of many kinds arose that the eighth century household could not withstand. Its passing created the tension and atmosphere of crisis Nilsson characterizes in his survey of the archaic period.

> Noch wichtiger ist die soziale Not der vorausgehenden Zeit, denn in irdischer Not richtet der Mensch seinen Sinn auf das Göttliche. Von den Göttern erwartet er Gerechtigkeit, Hilfe und Trost und den Trost sucht er in einer anderen Welt, wenn er ihn nicht auf Erden finden kann.[183]

In other words, revolutionary stress prompted the quest for some (literal) *ekstasis*.

Nilsson, in another analysis of the same phenomenon, writes at the beginning of the historic period religious ecstasy emerged with irresistible force.[184] The seventh century witnessed the nascence of experiential religion in this vein, the sixth century saw its full development. Nilsson continues:

> In the centuries preceding the Persian War, Greece presented a picture very unlike our ususal conception of the Hellenic world. Maenads in their ecstasy raged in the woods and fields...the land was full of prophets, wandering seers, collectors of oracles... By expiations and purifications plagues and epidemics were averted, contagious religious frenzies among hysterical women were conjured...that age seethed with religious unrest with new impulses and new ideas.[185]

That this was the age of the hero cult also is shown by Nilsson, in yet another study.

> It [scil. the cult of the hero] was developed during the dark age and the feuds of the petty Greek states in this age and in the beginning of the historical age

and his thesis is that when intercity strife made nonsense of rival claims on the protection of a shared god, such as Apollo, the Greeks turned to their local heroes for protection.

> Confined to their tombs and their country they [scil. the heroes] were the natural champions of their people and of nobody else.

Small anonymous local deities and landed gods[186] came back into prominence as well as newer, more robust personalities. In the games, predictably, they reappear. Adrastus at Nemea: and other heroes hitherto briefly mentioned, Melikertes and Palaimon at the Isthmia, Opheltes, Archemorus at Nemea; Heracles himself, the ἥρως *par excellence*,[187] certainly not absent at Nemea, but also prominent at the greatest and most sacred of the *agones*, Olympia.

Heracles is the hero of Olympia, and so at the center of the movement.[188] Pindar hails him again and again not solely as the founder of the festival, but more important as himself the Victor, for the occasion of the foundation of the games was Heracles' victory over the Moliones after the cleansing of the Augean stables. The Augean stables is the sixth and last of the Peloponnesian labors and in an early cycle may have been the last of Heracles' legendary labors altogether:[189] the games would then indeed be a joy, won not without struggle.[190] Heracles figures as Victor in the invocation of the second *Olympian* ode.

ἀναξιφόρμιγγες ὕμνοι
τίνα θεόν, τίν' ἥρωα, τίνα δ' ἄνδρα κελαδήσομεν;
ἤτοι Πίσα μὲν Διός · Ὀλυμπιάδα δ' ἔστασεν Ἡρακλέης
ἀκρόθινα πολέμου[191]

What man or god or hero, lyre,
Shall we this day acclaim?
Pisa is Zeus': Herakles'
Victor's and founder's fame.

Also in Archilochus' Victor's song, sung on the final day:

τήνελλα καλλίνικε χαῖρε ἄναξ Ἡράκλεις,
αὐτός τε καὶ Ἰόλαος, αἰχμητὰ δύο.
τήνελλα καλλίνικε χαῖρε ἄναξ Ἡράκλεις.[192]

It is not impossible that *the* hero,[193] the unnamed hero at

Olympia, is in fact to be understood as Heracles, in view of the latter's central position in the cult and the physical centrality of the former's altar.[194] At all events it is wrong to assume with Ziehen that the absence of a *temenos* or a sacrifice meant somehow a lack of cult; 'jedenfalls ist in O. selbst …von einem bedeutenderen Kult [scil. of Herakles] nichts zu finden.' This is to miss the wood for the trees with a vengeance, especially for a scholar who so amply recognizes the cultic aspect of the early games ('da standen Kulthandlung und Agon gleichbedeutend oder vielmehr der Agon war selbst eine Kulthandlung und wurde als solche gewertet'), for the actual contest was itself a cult of Heracles.[195]

Not that there were no altars or ceremonies for Heracles: discarding the Heracles of Ida for the propaganda he was, there were two altars to Heracles at Olympia,[196] of which one, significantly was to Heracles Παραστάτης, for here, as at Athens, Heracles was the companion, the pacemaker even, of the young men, with whom they drank in order to enter into communion with the god of strength and virility.[197] Other rites were ascribed to Heracles, not only the games themselves, but also the introduction of the wild olive and the celebration to Pelops, the local hero, Heracles' grandsire.[198] Pelops has been seen as more significant than Heracles at Olympia, but without reason, since there need to be no opposition in the aetiological story or in the exegesis.[199] Heracles sacrificed to Pelops as well as to Zeus means that when the agonistic cult of Heracles had taken root, other similar local cults attached themselves, notably that of Pelops.

Heracles, then, was the hero *par excellence*. Was it the agonistic cult that inspired the more general enthusiasm he received in the sixth century, or was it that his general popularity flowed back to Olympia to crystallize more sharply than before the image of the central hero of the agon? This was a process that, beginning with black-figure vase painting, was to be continued with the metopes of the temple of Zeus at Olympia and the paintings of Pheidias' brother, Panainos.[200]

If, now that the agonistic hero has been identified, and the profound motivation behind his connection with athletics has been located, the character of the archaic games ceremony is re-examined, an overwhelmingly religious quality emerges clearly. Indications of this are (1) the amount of time and importance given to ritual; (2) the archaizing quality of the ritual surrounding the athletic contest, 'der ja wie man nie vergessen darf eigentlich einen Teil des Kultes bildete';[201] (3) the violence of the events, which is not to be diagnosed as a symptom of oncoming professionalism or of thrill-seeking audiences, but was present and central from the start.

(1) *Ceremonial.* For a start, there was the ritual date of the event.[202] The festival was held at the time of the second or third full moon after the summer solstice, either in Apollonios or Parthenios, the seventh and eighth months respectively of the Elean Year, according to whether the four-year cycle was the first or second half of the eight-year calendar. The use of the Heraian cycle was deliberate archaizing, an illustration of what Eliade terms the recovery of 'illud tempus',[203] while the insistence on the full moon of high summer was also religious, the securing of a sacred time. The moonrise of the full moon, preceded by Pelops' sacrifice and followed by that to Zeus, was thus an integral episode in the ritual opening.[204]

Next, there was the nomenclature of the festival. So much is classed as ἱερόν: the agon itself, a distinction shared with the other Crown Games, the month of the agon, the persons of the athletes taking part.[205] The administrators of the truce (ἐκεχειρία) were designated officials of the temple of Zeus, and the purple-clad Hellanodicasts themselves (one till 580 B.C., thereafter two till the end of the fifth century) acted in archaic times much more as priestly examiners of the purity of athletes and the validity of the agon than as adjudicators in any technical sense as is shown, for example, in their judgement that Theagenes was to pay one talent to the treasury and one talent to Euthymus, his competitor in the pankration, for withdrawing from the field.[206] Their chief obligation (until bribery set in in the fifth century) was to scrutinize the claims of would-be participants to Greek descent and free birth, and to ensure that no one who had killed a man or defiled a temple took part.[207] The exclusion of married women from watching the contest (with the exeption of the priestess of Demeter Chlamyne) should reinforce the conception of the agon cult as Heracles' own, for women were generally excluded from his cult. Heracles was Μισογύνης, the woman-hater, just as he was Παλαίμων, the wrestler, the contender.[208]

Thirdly, the actual length of the ceremonial in early times is striking. In the eighth and early seventh century, by analogy with the Heraia,[209] it is probable that at the scattered occasions of the Kultakt, the only event was the stadion. The initial sacrifices to Pelops and Zeus will have taken much longer than the race, obviously. Later intermittent regularizing of the agon in the second half of the seventh century will have lengthened the duration of the festival to two and then to three days, the first of which was mainly ceremonial.[210] Still, the length of time spent on ceremony and the encirclement, as it were, of the athletics in a sacramental frame of such dimensions, is difficult to comprehend if the religious part of the festival were, as it became in Lucian's time, mere πάρεργον.[211] In the mid-fifth century, by which time the separating out of athletics from the cultic matrix was well advanced, the duration of the whole event may have been five days and so the proportion of time spent on sacrifice, oath-taking, procession, crowning, will in that case have been reduced to two-fifths, still a considerable fraction.[212] A day and a half of opening ceremony would be considered preposterous in a five-day fixture, once sport-for-sport's sake prevailed.

Finally, in this argument that the sixth century agones were on the one hand distinct from the funerary rites of Bronze Age chieftains and on the other different from the professionalized athletics they became, the ceremonial crowning of the victors is to be considered. The Olympic, Pythian, Nemean, and Isthmian Games were distinctly the Crown Games, ἀγῶνες στεφανῖται, in which a crown of some wild flora was the only award from the festival itself.[213] This striking fact must be interpreted in terms of cult and not obscured by reference to any distinction the victor's city awarded him. It should be noted also that in the rhapsodic contests, prizes both useful and valuable were awarded and in the occasional secular contest, 'after-dinner games', (no one is pretending they never happened),[214] the tripod was the regular award. Yet for the agon at Olympia the prize was a crown of wild olive (κότινος) picked ritually by a boy (ἀμφιθαλής) whose parents were both living, with a golden sickle, from the olive that Heracles brought to Olympia from

54

the Hyperboreans.[215] The crowning set the victor apart, signified his entry into the realm of joy and ease, the outward symbol of his fraternity with the immortal hero.

To be a crowned victor, to wear the olive, the bay, the celery, and the pine, set a man apart in the sixth century in a way inconceivable to writers preoccupied with the continuity of sport from Achilles onwards. Harris comments on this phenomenon inappropriately:

> At least we in our day have not yet reached a stage at which these darlings of the people are officially granted exemption from military service and other civic duties of the ordinary citizen.[216]

In fact the wearing of the crown was a sign that a man was even now in some sense apart, already a hero in his lifetime, certainly one after his death.[217] Hymns and statues, the prerogative of gods and heroes, were from an early date the reward of the victor: besides these, the civic privileges, the special seats, monetary grants, the frontline of battle, came as an anticlimax.[218] In the mysteries of Eleusis also the crown was ritually important, and these originated, as argued supra, in the same religious context as the agones. In such rites as these the wearer, whether animate or inanimate, was set apart, 'alles, was Kult und Verehrung genoss, bekränzte man demselben Gefühl heraus, Menschliches und Göttliches nicht unterscheidend'.[219] Cult, then, not sport, is the true description of the agon.

(2) *Archaizing*. Characteristic of a rite which in essence transports the participant from the profane to the sacred, is the impetus to archaize, to represent as anchored in remote antiquity that which may in fact be relatively recent. This nostalgia for the strong fresh pure world that existed *in illo tempore*[220] is especially noticeable in the account Pausanias gives of the evolution of the Olympic festival, dismissed by Ziehen as childish ('etwas naiven'),[221] but in fact a significant witness to the true nature of the event.

> When Iphitus renewed the games...people had forgotten the ancient customs, and they only gradually remembered them, and as they remembered them piece by piece, they added them to the games.[222]

55

Here Pausanias' vocabulary is telling: τῶν ἀρχαίων λήθη, ὁπότε τι ἀναμνησθεῖεν. So too with his references to the ancient writings of the Eleans — which as Mahaffy saw in fact refers to the calendar of Hippias of Elis, compiled at the close of the fifth century.[223] The tendency to archaize accounts for the absence of innovation in any marked degree: boys' classes of entrants were added, contests for heralds and trumpeters regularized; but even after the games were just games and little more, such sports as archery, swimming, any sort of ball game, quoits, hurdling, high jump, were not admitted.

There were, however, additions to the program at the end of the sixth century which are interesting for the light they cast on the direction the organizers of the late archaic period wanted the festival to take. These were the *hoplitodromos* (520 B.C.) and the κάλπη or trotting race for mares (496 B.C.).[224] In effect, since it has been argued that the whole festival was properly established only at the end of the seventh century, the *hoplitodromos* was the first innovation to be made. Gardiner argues that these races show the originally military nature of Greek athletics and were directly related to contemporary military developments.[225] In fact for the *diaulos* or two stades' race, all the competitors wore was a helmet, shield and greaves. A moment's reflection can assure the reader that this performance can have had no practical reference to hoplite warfare of the fifth century. Not only did the hoplite wear a heavy cuirass, but he also carried two spears and it has been argued — convincingly — that so clad he was never required to run, but at most to advance at quick march.[226] Further, the essence of hoplite fighting is the formation and maintenance of the line, as Tyrtaeus had impressed on the Spartans at the same period, as, it has been suggested, the agon cult began:[227] thus the cultic race and wrestling match began at the same moment that the military art turned away from the old virtues of élan and panache to discipline and tenacity as the ingredients of victory. Instead, the *hoplitodromos* was a symbol of the heroic past and the wearing of the bronze helmet a symbolic recall of the heroes for whom agility, hand-to-hand fighting, and fleetness of foot were, at least according to epic, the desiderata of the battlefield. It is significant that the *hoplitodromos* ended the whole festival: it was not a light-hearted finish (egg-and-spoon interpretation) nor a trailing off into insignificant events; it was a deliberate archaism, an evocation of the misty past of epic legend.[228]

So too with the κάλπη. In it, the rider on his mare trotted to a certain point, dismounted and ran with the horse to the finishing line. The performance lasted only thirteen Olympiads, from 496 B.C. to 444 B.C. Commentators, beginning with Pausanias, have noted the connection between the κάλπη and the ἀποβάται and correctly argued that both go back to the Homeric battle where the epic warriors drove to the affray and then dismounted. In other words, like the *hoplitodromos*, it was an archaism, an attempt to revive the inner ethos of a phenomenon going secular and technical.[229]

The fixed order of events also suggests a deliberate attempt to create a tradition. Pausanias' note of a single change in the order of events may be faulty and obscure:[230] but his intention certainly is to present the program as conservative while the evidence of the victors' lists also supports a fixed series: (1) equine events and pentathlon, (2) foot-races, (3) boxing and wrestling, (4) *hoplitodromos*; and within the category of foot-races, the same order of *dolichos, stade, diaulos*.[231]

Finally, as already noted, the elaborate calendar of the octaeteris that lies behind the calculation of the date of the Olympiads cannot be other than the affectation of the primitive for the sake of an atmosphere of greater antiquity. The Heraia used the octaeteris and according to Weniger the Olympic calendar will have deliberately archaized on this older model for the quadrennial festival even though the pentaeteris was current and in fact more suitable. But it lacked the aroma of high antiquity and so had no appeal.[232]

(3) *Violence.* Lastly in this demonstration that the Olympic *agon-fest* was essentially one whole Kultakt, the level of violence to be found in the contests and the brutality which marked the heavy-weight events is not without relevance. It does betray the true religious character of the phenomenon, for 'les dieux ont soif' and so must be fed with blood, sweat and tears.

For example, it is often said that the stadion (200 yards) was the prestige event, since the victor gave his name to the whole Olympiad, but this practice is no earlier than the third century B.C.[233] Nor does Plato's reference to the stadion in the *Laws* affect this assessment since *his* stasiodromos enters heavily armed.[234] Rather it was the παγκράτιον which in archaic times ranked as the premier event. ὁπόσα τέ ἐστιν ἐν ἀγωνίᾳ προτετίμηται πάντων τὸ παγκράτιον.[235]

Thucydides' two references to the Olympics both involve the winner of the παγκράτιον[236] and early victor lists make it clear that more victors in the παγκράτιον than the stade consistently thought it worthwhile recording the distinction.[237] Until the 470's all but a few records are of the παγκράτιον, and sufficient records are preserved to make it sure this is no accident.

But what then was the παγκράτιον which loomed so large in the estimate of the archaic Greeks? Harris objects to the description all-in wrestling; Marcus Aurelius, he argues, would not have commended the παγκράτιον if it had been merely brutal fighting.[238] The aim was to manoeuvre one's opponent into such a position that further resistence by him would involve his breaking a limb, having a joint dislocated, or being throttled. Biting and gouging the eyes were forbidden, otherwise no holds were barred. Naturally enough the mortality risk was high, as for example in the first certain mention by Pausanias, the victory of Arrichion of Phigaleia in 564 B.C.:

His adversary...got the first grip, and twining his legs above him held him fast while he squeezed his throat with his hands. Arrichion put one of his adversary's toes out of joint and expired under the grip that his adversary had on his throat, but the latter in the act of throttling was obliged at the same moment by the pain to give in. The Eleans crowned and proclaimed victorious the dead body of Arrichion.[239]

The manoeuvres of the παγκράτιον, ἀποστερνίζειν, γαστρίζειν, στρεβλοῦν make it clear that pain and injury if not death were an inseparable part of the contest, an agony indeed. This was the *agon* of Heracles when he slew the Nemean lion or wrestled with Triton, this the *agon* celebrated by Pindar in no fewer than 8 of the epinician odes.[240]

Contests of the northeast Peloponnese

The two athletic festivals of the northeast Peloponnese were modelled on Olympia. The Nemean and Isthmian games reproduce not only the events and order of Olympia, but also the inner core of struggle and survival, the central theme of aspiration towards the heroic, the experiential transcendence of individual existence.

Nemea. In some ways the Nemean games went beyond the Olympic agon. This seems to have been the case in archaizing, for example, since at Nemea alone the obscure *hippios* race was 800 yards, whereas elsewhere it was half the distance. Whattever the *hippios* was, it seems to have had an archaic connotation, perhaps a pony-tail type of helmet (as opposed to the crested helmet of the *hoplitodromos*) marked the race.[241]

But in most respects the Nemean games reflect rather than develop the Olympian pattern. The relation between Heracles and Pelops is repeated in the duality Heracles—Archemorus. The hypotheses d. and e. to Pindar's *Nemean Odes* both aver:

> Later on Heracles, victorious in the contest with the Nemean lion, took in hand the agon at Nemea and set it to rights, for in many ways it had fallen into disrepair.[242]

The tradition of a Heraclean foundation has again been married to the cult of a local hero, but whereas at Olympia the part by Pelops remained secondary, at Nemea, the role of Archemorus—Opheltes was enlarged and Heracles' part pushed from the front somewhat into the background.[243]

The reason for Heracles' eclipse and Archemorus' prominence should not surprise the reader of the previous section on Argive chauvinism. The Seven against Thebes, who, as we have seen, figured so prominently in Argive selfconsciousness, were, according to legend, saved by the child Opheltes—Archemorus inasmuch as he met his death through being bitten by a snake while his nurse drew water for the Seven. They in turn celebrated his funeral games which were the first Nemean games. Aeschylus' *Nemea* dealt with this story, so that by his day Heracles has clearly slipped into second place. A similar tendency is at work in the parallel legend that the first Nemean games were held at the funeral of Adrastus' brother Pronax and that Adrastus was the organizing hero, not Heracles. It will be remembered that this same Adrastus is the hero against whom Cleisthenes of Sicyon's

59

anti-Argive measures were directed. The contemporary elevation of Adrastus to the role of founder of the Nemean games was a direct riposte, an assertion of that uncompromising exclusiveness of Argos which so alienated her *adfines* in the area.[244]

It is for this reason that the description of the Crown Games as funerary has seemed more plausible at Nemea than elsewhere. The judges wore dark grey robes which the scholiasts construed as mourning apparel and the celery of the crown was considered a sign of death. Yet the celery crown is as likely to have been associated with Heracles: 'Hercules nunc populum capite praefert nunc oleastrum nunc apium.'[245] What we find is not so much an instance of funerary games as a local hero whose legend has been articulated with more than the usual explicitness. Heracles' struggles with the lion at Nemea are more in keeping with the ethos of the crown games phenomenon but such was the particularism of the Argives that Archemorus—Opheltes tended to edge him out. A comparable invasion of the agon cult, again the product of local tendencies, will be found at the Isthmia.

For distinctive sacrifices and ceremonial at the Nemean games, little evidence is forthcoming. Charles Williams' investigations have shown that what in 1925 Blegen took to be a crypt from first to last is in fact a fourth century crypt resting on the ground level of the previous temple: Blegen's remarks therefore about a subterranean holy of holies do not apply to archaic or classical times.[246] It is however noteworthy that this area within the temple was so carefully preserved exactly as it had been even though a crypt was thus necessitated. Williams notes the rough hewn appearance given to the room,[247] that it was a hallowed spot and the scene of some deeply felt ritual associated with the agon is certain, possibly a second-oath-taking to Archemorus following upon that to Zeus, as Broneer has suggested happened in the Palaimonion at the Isthmia.[248]

For the actual conduct of the games there is again little evidence of departure from the Olympian paradigm. Not only the *hippios* but also the *hoplitodromos* was run over 800 yards, a unique length for this exacting race, and Gardiner felt they became a special feature of the Nemea.[249] Is this fact to be construed as support for Farnell's otherwise fragile assertion that the Nemea was partly an Argive military festival?[250] It is more probable that, as with the *hippios* race, the long *hoplitodromos* is evidence of a desire to archaize distinctly and to create an atmosphere singularly Argive.

Isthmia. At Corinth as at Nemea, the Isthmian games were in themselves a faithful reflection of the Olympian pattern: the same events, the same order of events, was the rule; for the so-called regatta, sometimes listed as the distinguishing feature of the Isthmian games, was clearly a literary fiction.[251] Yet an atmosphere different from Olympia reveals itself persistently in the descriptions we have of the scene and in the details of its religious patronage. This difference Gardiner explains by reference to Corinth's bustling and cosmopolitan character, [252] but can we *just* read back Aelius Aristides and Dio Chrysostom into the early sixth century B.C.? If not, then the singularities of the Isthmian celebration, the mystic and dionysiac side of proceedings must be derived from elsewhere, from the mythology surrounding the institution of the games, and the contemporary culture of the community.

In line with Olympian and Nemean parallels, it is supposed that the late seventh century saw the spontaneous rise of an agon cult centered on a hero, in this case not Heracles but Theseus. So Plutarch: 'He [Theseus] also instituted the games [scil. the Isthmian games] in emulation of Heracles', and the hypothesis to Pindar's *Isthmians*, 'Some say he instituted the Isthmian agon on the occasion of his victory over Sinis', while Plutarch had earlier commented that Theseus destroyed Sinis as ὁ Πιτυοκάμπτων had destroyed others to show that strength surpasses technique. But by the late seventh century this Theseus will have been definitely Athenian and not simply the local *kouros* of the Isthmian region that Will conjectures. When the Corinthians came to regularize the agon on a permanent basis, the Athenian protagonist was unwelcome.[253]

There followed a compromise, it is supposed, in which for the grant of προεδρία in perpetuity, the Athenian Theseus withdrew and the official launching on a permanent biennial basis in 585 B.C. associated the games not with Theseus, but with Palaimon. The official foundation legend, repeated in hypothesis c. to Pindar's *Isthmian* odes, held that Ino, driven out of her wits by her mad husband, Athamas, having thrust one son into a cauldron of boiling water, fled with the other,

61

Melikertes, and so came to the Isthmus of Corinth. At this point her husband caught up with her, but she, to evade him, leapt into the sea and was drowned, together with her son, and while she became the sea nymph Leukothea, her son became Palaimon and, being washed ashore on a dolphin's back, was found by Sisyphus king of Corinth. Either prompted by a Nereid or by his own wit, Sisyphus held the first Isthmian contest at the interment of the drowned Palaimon, and, prompted again by the Nereids, made the funeral ceremony into a periodic event.[254]

Will's examination of this legend isolates an interesting aspect of the Palaimon cult. In Ino, he sees a vegetation spirit, a *kourotrophos* associated with Dionysus (his nurse often) and a giver of oracles, while Melikertes, he suggests, was the central figure in a tree cult, that is, the spirit of a pinetree or grove of pinetrees. Leukothea, on the other hand, Will explains as an *hypostasis* of Aphrodite anadyomene, honoured in many parts of the Aegean, though Palaimon the son is known only at the Isthmus, except for a doubtful instance at Tenedos. The syncretism of these dyads, one of the land, one of the sea, produced a cult in which the grief and lamentation ($\vartheta\rho\tilde{\eta}\nu o\varsigma$, $\pi\acute{\epsilon}\nu\vartheta o\varsigma$) of the dionysiac agrarian ritual, expressed by night and in underground mystery rites, became in myth the wailing of Leukothea for her son Palaimon drowned in the deeps.[255]

Thus to this chthonic fertility cult, whose protodionysiac elements of dirge and orgy ($\vartheta\rho\tilde{\eta}\nu o\varsigma\ldots\tau\epsilon\lambda\acute{\epsilon}\sigma\tau\iota\kappa o\varsigma\ \tau\epsilon\ \kappa\alpha\grave{\iota}$ $\acute{\epsilon}\nu\vartheta\epsilon o\varsigma$[256]) had been accentuated by syncretism with the marine dyad Leukothea—Palaimon, there was now added the cult of the agonistic hero, and Leukothea's son may only now have taken the name Palaimon, characteristic of the archetypal agon hero Heracles.[257] The older cult, however, while permeating the new, maintained sufficient independence of it to be able to go on, even when the agon cult was at least partially subtracted from it:[258] the pinetree, in particular, present in both Sinis and Palaimon myths, and central to the exegesis of Melikertes' nature, did not owe its significance at the Isthmus solely or even primarily to the fact that the first agon crowns were made from it. Melikertes —Palaimon maintained a powerful presence at the Isthmus separable from his role as hero of the games. His rites, altars, symbols (pine) dominated the scene, while

Theseus as we have seen, was never wholly eclipsed.

It was the Melikertes—Palaimon cult, then, with which the Isthmian games were chiefly associated when they were in-augurated or systematised in 589. It has been suggested earlier that Periander or his successor hoped to acquire in Sisyphus, the burier of Palaimon, the type of venerable elder hero that Pelops was for Olympia, and that this hope foundered on the rejection by Corinthian culture of the quasi-historical legend in preference to the genuine mythical heroes.[259] The way in which Palaimon developed as the dead son of the goddess will reinforce the impression of an auto-nomous spirituality and emotional receptivity among the Corinthians. For not only did renewed interest in Leukothea (hypostasis of Aphrodite) harmonize with the development in the sixth century of Cyprian Aphrodite's cult in Corinth,[260] but the figure of Palaimon also syncretized naturally with the new fifth century form of Rhea-worship, the Pessinuntine cult of Cybele, Mother of the Gods. Melikertes—Palaimon, violently drowned and ritually mourned in proto-dionysiac orgies, had much in common with Attis, *paredros* of the Great Mother Cybele, himself closely associated with the pine-tree, who died violently and was then mourned with the wild ritual lamentation of the *archigalli*:[261] here we may really see elements of the ritual *leichenspiele*. Some of the features of later Palaimon worship seem to be drawn from the Cybele cult: the torchbearers, illustrated for the rites of Attis by the torchbearing maiden of conventional iconography and for Palaimon by the singular lamp stands found by Broneer at the Isthmus and used for the nocturnal celebration of Palai-mon; and also the continued centrality of the pine at the Isthmus, even when, as will appear, the victors' wreaths were of wild celery.[262] It was the ability to syncretize that effec-ted this autonomy of cult. The religious life of the Isthmus had a self-renewing vitality independent of the games, and in this way, here as at Nemea, the character of the host culture affected the modification of the Olympian agon and the cult of the agonistic hero.

Apart from the orgia the Isthmian games may have evinced a greater tendency to experiment technically than is apparent at Olympia or Nemea. The early introduction of an inter-mediate category of competitors, and in a different direction, the fifth century invention of the *husplex* for starting the runners,[263] point to an early professionalism at Corinth, which would be the reflection in sport of that precocious secularity which has been indicated in politics, and is indeed the natural partner to Corinth's predilection for the ecstatic and mysterious modality of the sacred.

This chapter has sought to show that the crown contests, the ἀγῶνες στεφανῖται which arose sporadically towards the end of the eighth century, grew in importance in the seventh, and were regularized and institutionalized in the sixth, were not in fact games as we know them, but rather hero cults, focused on the central figure of an agonistic hero, through whose toils, repeated by his votaries, immortality, existential immortality, was achieved. Only so can the part played by this particular form of the cult be understood, for on the one hand, such a cult ideally suited an age when the individual was for the first time realizing his identity distinct from the collective unit, and on the other, it is clear that the Greeks, no more than anyone else, gave no extraordinary metaphysical veneration to the performance of any kind of sport in and of itself.

To view the agon cult in this light explains something which has hitherto been found difficult, that is, Pindar's lack of interest in the sporting events he commemorates. Pindar is the spokesman of the games, yet seems wholly uninterested in their detail. He is in fact the last exponent of the ideology of the agon cult, and is already aware that secularism (mere training, διδάκται ἀρέται) is permeating athletics as so much else in fifth century Greece.[264] Bowra repeatedly stresses Pindar's preoccupation with the heroic ideal:

> This [scil. N. 1.69–72] illustrates at the highest imaginable level what victory means to a man after he has won it. It is a lasting joy, a wonderful relief, a proper compensation for his efforts, and above all it is a fulfilment of his youthful gifts and promise, the best that he can have hoped for in his first eager prime.[265]

But the context Bowra gives the hero is worldly and secular, consisting of fame, renown, and success, which is implausible when even a conservative interpretation of the religious context is remembered. It is not fame and honour but life and reality which beckon the hero, in Finley's phrase 'the flash of the gods in this world'.[266]

τὸ δὲ παθεῖν εὖ πρῶτον ἄθλων· εὖ δ᾽ ἀκούειν δευτέρα μοῖρ᾽...[267]

So also should Q.1.93 be explained:

τὸ δὲ κλέος
τηλόθεν δέδορκε τᾶν Ὀλυμπιάδων ἐν δρόμοις
Πέλοπος, ...
ὁ νικῶν δὲ λοιπὸν ἀμφὶ βίοτον
ἔχει μελιτόεσσαν εὐδίαν
ἀέθλων γ᾽ ἕνεκεν· τὸ δ᾽ αἰεὶ παράμερον ἐσλὸν
ὕπατον ἔρχεται παντὶ βροτῶν.

It is not, as Farnell suggests, euhemerism that impels Pindar to extol the present moment, but it is the priority of the immediate, existential victory, contrasted with later renown, (ὁ νικῶν again, contrasted with τὸ κλέος) the experiential immortality which is the prize of toil. Taken in Farnell's sense, the interjection interrupts the sense, but taken in the manner suggested τὸ δ᾽ αἰεὶ παράμερον ἐσλὸν is but an explanation of μελιτόεσσα εὐδία: honey-sweet well-being, existential immortality, ὕπατον meaning the ultimate in degree.[268]

The Dioscuri, Pelops, Tlepolemus, Bellerophon, Oenomaus, the roll-call of heroes is lengthy, yet Heracles for Pindar too, as for the painters, is the supreme hero. *Olympians* 2 (ἀναξιφόρμιγγες ὕμνοι) and *Olympians* 10 (ἄπονον δ᾽ ἔλαβον χάρμα παῦροί τινες) have already been cited for Heracles' deathless ease and the founding of the games. Elsewhere, Heracles' name is never far.

It is Heracles' reward on Olympus,[269] the bright glitter of joy, the presence of youth and the immortals that Pindar speaks of, as well as the strength[270] and resolve that achieved this blessed state; and Pindar speaks, too, as if Heracles and the other victors were intermediaries between gods and men, able, as heroes are, to procure for others the valour[271] that will bring them the forgetfulness of pain (λήθη πόνων) and the enjoyment of unending pleasure.

εἰ γάρ τις ἀνθρώπων δαπάνᾳ τε χαρείς
καὶ πόνῳ πράσσει θεοδμάτους ἀρετάς,
σύν τέ οἱ δαίμων φυτεύει δόξαν ἐπήρατον ἐσχατιαῖς ἤδη πρὸς ὄλβου
βάλλετ᾽ ἄγκυραν θεότιμος ἐών.

65

For if a man expends himself in the
Struggle and wins heroic stature,
If the God then grant him glory and honour,
He is divine and to him belongs the ultimate in ecstasy.[272]

Chapter IV

CORINTH AND THE OLD POLITICS

Paradoxically, in view of previous argument to demonstrate the modernity of Corinthian politics and the spontaneity of Corinthian cult, it was Corinth not Argos which, in the transitional period, made a bid for the hegemony of the northeast Peloponnese on the basis of the old politics of seers and ceremonies. The paradox is resolved, however, by the fact that this departure was uncharacteristic, a panic-stricken reaction to Athenian provocation. The bid to unite at least the northern half of the region, from Cleonae and Phlius up to the Isthmus and Megara, failed completely, so much so that little trace of the whole manoeuvre remains in the sources. Were it not that epigraphy underwrites part of the story, the miscellany of scholia and anecdote of which the reconstruction is built would hardly bear its weight. But before the action taken by Corinth in these years is outlined, the situation which prompted her so to act should be considered.

The Athenian challenge

Prior to the Persian Wars Corinth's attitude to Athens was friendly.[273] Athenian policy towards Corinth however grew steadily more hostile and by 479 Athens stood as a grave and undisguised threat to Corinth's continuing status as a polis of any significance in the Greek world. On the Serpent Column[274] erected after Plataea the inscription ran:

Corinth's chances of maintaining this parity were lessening by the month.

Number of ships. The key to Corinth's anxieties lay in the spectacular growth of the Athenian fleet from a respectable 50 in 487 B.C. to a grand total of 271 in 480 B.C.[275] This incomparable naval force burst on the Greek political scene within a short space of time, for the *psephismata* of Themistocles, assigning the silver from Maroneia (Laurion) to the construction of a trireme fleet, were not passed before 483.[276] Herodotus' figures, imperfect though they may be, can be bolstered by Thucydides' clear, unequivocal observation that, prior to Xerxes' invasion of Greece, the leading seapowers of the 480's, Aegina and Athens, had negligible naval forces, and the total of 50 for Athens and 70 for Aegina shows us what Thucydides meant by negligible.[277] In 480 B.C. Corcyra, with only 60 ships, ranked as the second Greek naval power while Aegina, also claiming second place, had a fleet which the most arbitrary inclusion of reserves in home waters cannot raise past 50. Thus although there are grounds for raising Corinth's total, still, 40 or not, neither Corinth nor Corcyra nor Aegina were at all comparable with Athens' 271: not even with Athens having only a round 200 if Labarbe's close argumentation is rejected.[278] Two years thus saw Athens outbuild the rest by a sufficiently wide margin for her naval preponderance to be assured for several years. Corinth, whose round ships may even have carried to Piraeus the timber from southern Italy for this crash program of shipbuilding,[279] viewed its outcome with dismay, dismay that increased as the Athenians emerged from 480 B.C. not only immensely superior in the numbers of their triremes but openly and vindictively hostile to Corinth.

The originality ($\varphi \acute{v} \sigma \epsilon \omega \varsigma$ $\grave{\iota} \sigma \chi \acute{v} \varsigma$) with which Thucydides credits Themistocles lay not only in the construction of a fighting fleet as such and on such a scale, but principally in Themistocles' appreciation of the political uses of a navy as a new factor in the Greek world.[280] The Ionians had mustered 353 triremes at Lade; the Thasians had made an all-out effort to build a trireme fleet and city defences to go with it; but in both cases the initiative lay outside, whereas Themistocles' fleet, though used against the Persians, was not built as a defensive but an offensive striking arm.[281] It is not too much to say that in abandoning the relationship between fighting ships and merchant marine, pentekonters and round ships, hitherto the rule, Themistocles had moved Greece forwards into an era of technical specialized war at sea as far from the archaic naukraries as Cleisthenes' political transformation was from their civilian counterparts, the early demes.

The Corinthians and Aeginetans, the principal merchant marine of the early fifth century, had not perceived the uses of a large trireme fleet: expensive to build, difficult to man, useful solely for fighting (unlike the pentekonters), the triremes' numbers were kept down to an establishment no larger than necessary to protect the round ships. Athens' shipbuilding produced alarm and resentment. As early as the winter 481/480 B.C.[282] there had been talk of entrusting the Athenians with the command at sea, but the allies were averse to the plan, and by July 480 the appointment of the Lacedaemonian Eurybiades to command the fleet followed from the declaration of the allies that if a Lacedaemonian did not take the command, they would break up the fleet, for never would they serve under the Athenians.[283] As the campaign of 480 went on, Herodotus' narrative shows Adeimantus the Corinthian continually at Eurybiades' elbow and, as the Corinthian contingent was more than double Sparta's, it is reasonable to infer that 'the allies' who resisted Athens' claim were led by the Corinthians.[284] Eurybiades indeed seems to have been caught in the crossfire of Athenian and Corinthian strategies and his replacement by Leotychidas, the Eurypontid Spartan king, may reflect Corinth's insistence on an admiral prepared to take a firmer stand against Themistocles' pressure.[285] The failure of Themistocles' plan for a naval offensive in 479 B.C., if this is what his absence from Herodotus' narrative implies, suggests that Leotychidas listened more attentively to Corinth's insistence on the naval defence of the Saronic Gulf coming first: hence their station at Aegina throughout the spring months before cautiously moving on, first to Delos, and then to Samos in August 479 B.C.[286] Leotychidas' rapport with the Peloponnesian elements of the fleet, not the Spartans alone, is significant for the later movement of the ships, in particular for their wintering over (in 479/78 B.C.) in Thessaly.

The Corinthians thus seem to have adopted an attitude of suspicion and resentment of Themistocles, as the author of Athens' sudden and overwhelming naval superiority. The envy and hatred of which Herodotus and Plutarch speak erupted nowhere more virulently than at the Isthmus, when at the *aristeia* (award of honours) in 480 B.C. the representatives of the other sea-going cities united in their refusal to award Themistocles first place: ready enough to recognize his ability on the eve of the battle, they would not, on reflection, applaud his position or policy, preferring, according to Herodotus, not to make any award at all.[287] Such was the mood at the Isthmus where Corinth's influence would be most felt.

Propaganda. This resentment and suspicion could only be increased by Themistocles' anti-Corinthian propaganda. Hignett has trenchantly argued that all attempts to explain away as misunderstood manoeuvre or deliberate feint the rumoured disappearance of the Corinthian ships from the Greek line at Salamis are misdirected. If the story of their disappearance was maliciously intended, why cannot it have been a complete fabrication without any foundation whatever? he asks. His own view is that the Corinthian ships fought throughout the battle on the right wing next to the Spartans, so as to balance the strong Athenian force on the left, and that in this position they held off the Persian left, the Ionians, and so were instrumental in blocking the retreat of the Persian right, the Phoenicians, as they fled towards Phaleron.[288]

When was this story put about? As late as 432 B.C. when Adeimantus' son would have been identifiable as an enemy of Athens? After 452 B.C. when Thucydides says Corinthian hatred of Athens reached a new intensity after the Athenian alliance with Megara?[289] Or, surely, in the period following the battle when the part played by each state was being reconstructed, when the awards for valour for cities and individuals were being decided, an episode Herodotus reports immediately before the story of the Corinthian panic and flight. As Whatley has acutely shown, allegations and counter-allegations of this kind, while hotly debated as soon as hostilities end, are only finally cleared up when reputations have no longer to be saved.[290] Thus it is precisely the immediate post-war scene which sees exaggerated rumours in circulation. In 452 B.C., moreover, it was the Corinthians whose animosity was exacerbated while the Athenians would have preferred to cool the situation. The circulation of the story of Corinthian cowardice reflects not Corinth's but Athen's animosity. Herodotus directly attributes the tale to the Athenians and adds that the rest of Greece joined Corinth in repudiating it.

This was not the first time the Athenians had maligned the Corinthian fleet. At Artemision, so the rumour ran, both the Spartan and the Corinthian admirals had to be bribed to stay and fight, and when retreat was in order it was, sure enough, then that the Corinthians led the way. These stories are dismissed by Hignett as 'pure invention', and so they are, but not of Herodotus' making.[291] They must be interpreted as part of an anti-Corinthian propaganda, put about after the seabattles of 480 B.C. to establish beyond doubt the unrivalled superiority of Athens, when Corinth, once thalassocrat herself, could be seen to have fallen so low.

Corcyra and Aegina. Athen's next move was not propagandist but political. It is to the post-Salamis period, the period so well caught by Timocreon (restoring people here, expelling there) that Themistocles' arbitration in favour of the Corcyreans against Corinth may be held to belong.[292] The twenty talents penalty levied on Corinth was a heavy fine and to have her hold on her colonial territories compromised a no less serious blow. Corcyra's 60 triremes, it has already been noted, represented the second largest fleet after the Athenian engaged in the 480 campaign, though not actually present at Salamis. The situation mirrors that of 433 B.C.: then Corcyra warned the Athenians against letting the fleets of Corinth and Corcyra coalesce; in 479/78 B.C. it was Corinth who had to fear a Corcyra-Athens coalition brought about on Athens' initiative.

Corcyra's *rapprochement* with Athens is uncontroversial. A more tenuous *entente* may be reconstructed in the case of Aegina. Were she also to gravitate to Athens'

71

side, two of the three second-rank navies of Greece would then be aligned with the new superpower. Meiggs has recently reargued the untenability of Aegina in the Delian League in 478: but he has also shown the extensive coincidence of interest between the two states, the common profit for both in a diminished Persian empire. Accordingly Wickert's suggestion of an entente (ξύμμαχοι) without formal membership of the Delian League is attractive.[293] What could be done to counter the increasing pressure Athens was bringing to bear on her erstwhile ally and to restore the prestige and influence that had been Corinth's?

The Corinthian response

Corinth's solution was to capitalize on the opportunity offered by Argos' eclipse to create a zone of influence among the small city states of the north east Peloponnese; to actualize the potential for unity long offered by the arterial highway she dominated from the north. Pressed by the maritime power she turned to the not inconsiderable advantages of territory and situation she enjoyed on the landward side[294] and adopted a policy of territorial hegemony on the basis of Dorian tradition and heritage. As Sparta had turned her claim to be Achaean to good purpose in 510 B.C., so Corinth in 480 asserted her title to be known as a major Dorian landed state.

Nemea. She began, it is argued, by invading the territory of Cleonae and usurping the presidency of the Nemean Festival; this was only possible in the face of total inertia and maximum eclipse on the part of Argos, for, as has been shown, the Nemean games were essentially an Argive festival even if the Cleonaeans under their protection were titular prsidents. This Corinthian campaign is sufficiently obscure to necessitate a complete statement of the evidence that it ever happened.

(1) Two of the scholiasts to Pindar's Nemean Odes record an episode of Corinthian presidency. Hypothesis c. states

προέστησαν δὲ τοῦ ἀγῶνος καὶ Ἀργεῖοι καὶ
Κορίνθιοι καὶ Κλεωναῖοι

and hypothesis d.,

προέστησαν δὲ τοῦ ἀγῶνος μὲν
Κλεωναῖοι, εἶτα Κορίνθιοι.[295]

Thus hypothesis c.'s order is: Argives, Corinthians, Cleonaeans, while hypothesis d. gives Cleonaeans, Corinthians. Therefore the scholiasts were not using the same list and need not be treated as one authority. Neither scholiast's argument is particularly impressive in its own right: c., who quotes Aeschylus (on a different point), is perhaps sounder than d., to whom we owe the misinformation that the Isthmian crowns were of withered celery and the Nemean crowns of fresh, a comment not worth the credence given to it by Broneer.[296] On the other hand a historical note in the scholia is not necessarily as unreliable as fanciful glosses on myth or legend. For what it is worth, then, the two scholiasts seem to know of a period of Corinthian presidency and one of them, c., puts this before the final Cleonaean, that is Argive, restoration in the mid-fifth century.

(2) Plutarch, in his life of Cimon, records an anecdote of Cimon's riposte to the Corinthian Lachartos who challenged the Athenian's right to cross Corinthian territory uninvited. People who knock at doors, said he, do not go in before the owner bids them. To which Cimon replied,

> Are you in any position to criticize, Lachartos? You Corinthians did not knock at the gates of Cleonae and Megara but broke them down; you forced your way into those cities by force of arms, and claimed that the right of way was always due to the wielders of superior military power.

> ('ἀλλ' οὐχ ὑμεῖς,' εἶπεν, 'ὦ Λάχαρτε, τὰς Κλεωναίων καὶ Μεγαρέων πύλας κόψαντες ἀλλὰ κατασχίσαντες εἰσεβιάσασθε μετὰ τῶν ὅπλων ἀξιοῦντες ἀνεῳγέναι πάντα τοῖς μεῖζον δυναμένοις.')

Meyer's assumption that not one but two separate incidents are involved coheres with the obvious fact that Megara and Cleonae lie in different directions from Corinth — so probably two expeditions are meant. It would not be relevant here to analyse the Megarian reference: Meyer took the context to be 'bald nach dem Kriege', the Persian war, that is, 'als Megara wieder einmal mit Korinth in Grenzstreitigkeiten

73

geriet'. This then is an early move in the story of Megara's turning towards the Athenian alliance, a story which culminated in Myronides' defeat of the Corinthians in the Megarid in 457 B.C.[297]

When we turn to Cleonae it must be admitted that any dating will be arbitrary given the paucity of the evidence: this does not preclude the consideration of this episode *as part of* the total conjecture here presented. Wilamowitz — and Busolt — give a date post 464 B.C. because of the mention of Ion in the preceding paragraph in Plutarch but this assumption is itself not beyond criticism.[298] To what other episode then might Cimon be taken to refer? He was speaking in 461 B.C. on his return from the ill-starred expedition in aid of Sparta: are we to infer, as Wilamowitz did, that the Corinthian assault on Cleonae (and Megara) took place shortly before this, so as to give the repartee greater pungency and appositeness? How far back would an angry Athenian go in listing Corinthian aggression on her neighbours? Meyer, for one, felt that 10 or 11 years was a possible interval when he linked this passage in Plutarch with the inscription (Hill's *Sources* no. 110) and set both in the late 470's.[299] Further back than this, it may be felt, political memory does not reach, not for the purpose of trading insults at any rate. So Dow writes: 'The defiant statement by Kimon should refer to an event recent enough to be vivid in everyone's mind', and a gap of more than 11 years is felt to be awkwardly long.[300]

But this restraint is unnecessary. In the opening episodes of the Peloponnesian war, according to Thucydides who is trying to write plausibly, the Corinthians go back 45 years without a qualm in citing the aid they gave Athens in 487 B.C. against Aegina, and the Plataeans also, pleading with the Spartans in 427, go back 35 even 92, years in expecting instant familiarity with the events of the past on the part of their interlocutors. Further, in the context of a political feud between Athens, and Corinth, such as has been suggested for the period of the Persian Wars and the post-war decades, it is not necessary even to posit familiarity with the events on the part of the general public: the antagonists can be relied on to keep alive any relevant episode. A date in the early postwar period — 476 B.C. will be suggested — made plausible by the opportunity Argos' eclipse afforded, is not weakened by the immediate context of Plutarch's anecdote being in 461.[301]

(3) Last, there is the epigraphic evidence already mentioned of Hill's *Sources* no. 110, τὰργ[ει]οι ἀνέθεν τόι Διὶ τõυ Φορωθόθεν.[302] Hill gives a queried date of c. 460. Forrest would place the dedication earlier, towards the opening years of the decade.[303] It represents, it may be argued, the repression by Argos of this Corinthian policy of expansion and the end of the short-lived local ascendancy Corinth had sought. Meyer indeed seems to place the inscription earlier still at the end of the 470's, where he also sets the Plutarch *Cimon* 17 anecdote, but there is no necessity to suppose that Argive reaction followed instantly upon Corinthian aggression.[304] All that must happen is that the sequence Corinth's move/ Argive response must be maintained and thus the Plutarch reference gives a terminus for the inscription, if indeed the two are allowed to be connected.

These three items: the scholia, the passage in Plutarch, the Argive dedication, thus suggest a Corinthian capture of Nemea, following a campaign against Cleonae of some violence, then a period of Corinthian presidency of the games, and finally ejection of Corinth by Argos at a date in the late 470's or early 460's, closing the whole episode.

It should be noted that the excavators of Nemea have expressed some scepticism about the existence of this period of Corinthian presidency. Miller,[305] who recovered IG IV.484 — an inscription, from Nemea, of the right date i.e. 460's, with a distinctively Corinthian ε, felt that it might simply be the work of a good Corinthian cutter frequenting the panhellenic festivals in search of commissions. It is a possible account, but I think hypercritical, and in more recent years the abundance of fifth century Corinthian roof tiles might perhaps be used to provide the *tangible* evidence of a Corinthian presence which Miller at first felt to be lacking.

If, however, we accept Corinth's intervention, the character of this policy deserves comment in the light of the previous characterization of Corinthian culture in the archaic period as being in matters of cult spontaneous, and in politics emancipated and secularizing. The abuse of myth for political ends failed at Corinth, succeeded at Argos, was characteristic of Argos, unnnatural for Corinth. Further, in a transitional period, when the old determinants of politics (shrines, relics, games) were fading and the new (opposing political ideologies) were coming in, can it be Corinth which espoused the old style of politics in wresting the presidency of the Nemean games from Cleonae, Argos which took up the new mode via synoecism and a democratic league? The irony is attributable, it is argued here, to the catalytic presence of Themistocles, panicking the Corinthians into futile historicism, cajoling the Argives into unfamiliar liberal ways.

The celery crown. Corinth, however, did more than take over the Nemean festival. Once secure in the presidency, she attempted to gratify and reconcile the affronted Cleonaeans by changing her own Isthmian crown from pine to celery, so that the Nemean crown, Heracles' (Doric) crown, the Nemean celery, was now in use in *both* agonistic festivals in the area. This striking gesture affirming Corinth's Dorianism *without parallel elsewhere*, was a bold move in her campaign to win the allegiance of the northeast Peloponnese. It failed because the significance of such gestures was diminishing and because the Corinthians themselves seem to have been disinclined to maintain the Dorian mode of which the celery crown from Nemea was the symbol. The crown itself, however, they did not discard, and it would be over 500 years before they went back to the original pine crown.

The change of crown and its date must now be substantiated. That the earliest Isthmian crown was pine, was unknown to the scholiasts on Pindar's Isthmian odes, who only know the succession celery-pine. Plutarch, however, is aware that the recent ($\chi\vartheta\acute{\epsilon}\varsigma$) change to pine was a revival, not an innovation, and his quoted evidence is Callimachus, Euphorion, and Procles. The last two indeed, as authors of specialist treatises on the Isthmian games from the third century B.C., could be considered good authorities on this point.[306] In addition, there is the evidence of the fragment from Aeschylus' satyr play *Theoroi* or *Isthmiastai*, of which 98 verses survive.[307] Verses 75–76 of Snell's reconstruction of the fragment run:

σὺ δ᾽ ἰσθμιάζεις καὶ πίτυος ἐστ[εμμένος]
κλάδοισι, κισσοῦ δ᾽ οὐδ[α]μου τιμη[ν ἔχων].

But you are now participants in the Isthmians: the
Pine bough on your head, you just despise the ivy.[308]

Thus Dionysus (the speaker) reproaches the chorus of satyrs

76

for abadoning his rites and turning to new celebrations.[309] It follows that the audience hearing the play will have been at least familiar with the existence of pine crowns at the Isthmus, which will either still be in vogue or have been discarded within living memory. To the audience of the *Isthmiastai* the pine crown at the Isthmian games must be a familiar idea for the line to have point.

More might be extracted from the papyrus fragments than the mere fact of a pine crown in an earlier epoch. What is the play about after all but *an exchange of crowns*, a transfer of patronage, a new look at the Isthmian festival? It might have been argued once that the prominence of the chorus suggested an early date for the play, as far back as the 490's, but the implications of the papyrus list of victors in the tragic contests, which necessitate a late date for the 50-chorus *Suppliants*, have told in favour of Nestle's original argument that a key role in the drama for the chorus indicates a later rather than an earlier dating, after 480 B.C. rather than before.[310] It could be conjectured that the *Isthmiastai* was in fact partly aimed at the Corinthian manoeuvre: a play about fickle Corinthians changing crowns from ivy to pine might be intended as a gibe at the solemn reconsecration the Corinthians intended by their adoption of celery for pine. The line on pine crowns ran:

σὺ δ᾽ ἰσθμιάξεις καὶ πίτυος ἐστεμμένος

An earlier line, foreshadowing it, and providing the key to the drama, is v. 34 which runs:

σὺ δ᾽ ἰσθμιάξεις καὶ τρόπους και[νοὺς μ]αθών

The theme is repeated later, v. 85:

ἐπεὶ τ]ὰ καινὰ ταῦτα μα[νθά]νειν φιλεῖ[ς

says Sisyphus and goes on to explain the use of strange new objects won from axe and anvil, by which, Snell suggests, Sisyphus means the javelin for the pentathlon, invented, like so much else, at Corinth, or so it is being claimed.

As to the date of the play,[311] di Marco, whose excellent treatment stresses the theme of cultures in conflict, Athenian and Corinthian (and, I would say, old and new Corinthian), hazards a date after the poet's (first) Sicilian visit, arguing from the masks which the Satyrs in the play affix to the temple: this was a practice widely followed in contemporary Sicily.[312]

It is Pindar, however, who may give not only a terminus ante quem for the change of crowns but also evidence as to the intention behind it. Pindar, according to Dow, is writing as the Corinthians would have him, willing to repeat the Corinthian propaganda.[313] Celery, Pindar insists, is the material of the Isthmian crown, and he writes as if there had never been any other, which must be propaganda: Aeschylus' audiences are familiar with the now rejected pine. It was one and the same generation which listened to Pindar's odes and Aeschylus' tragedies.

Pindar refers four times to the Isthmian crown of celery: *O.* 13.33, *N.* 4.88, *I.* 2.16, *I.* 8.64. The dating of the earliest of these, viz. *I.* 8, is the subject of an argument by Finley in which the year 478 B.C. is posited as the most likely year for the ode in question.

> If I. 8 follows a victory in the early spring of 478 B.C., the time would fit Pindar's deeply divided and troubled sense of past pain and present, still hesitant relief.[314]

The reference is to vv. 9–11:

ἐπειδὴ τὸν ὑπὲρ κεφαλᾶς
τὸν Ταντάλου λίθον παρά τις ἔτρεψεν ἄμμι θεός,
ἀτόλματον Ἑλλάδι μόχθον.

> For the gods have rolled away the stone of Tantalus
> That hung above our heads
> The bane and scourge of Hellas.

This nightmare passed away (δεῖμα παροιχόμενον[315]) is the Persian menace, so the ode postdates Salamis 480 B.C. and Plataea 479 B.C. At v. 63 the second person honoured in the ode besides the Isthmian victor Cleander is introduced, Cleander's cousin Nicocles, the boxer, now dead, and we are bidden:

...γεραίρετέ νιν, ὅς ῞Ισθμιον ἂν νάπος
Δωρίων ἔλαχεν σελίνων.

Honour ye him who once within the Isthmian glade
Secured the Dorian crown of celery.

Since Nicocles won a celery crown at the Isthmus, celery
crowns must have been awarded at an Isthmian festival earlier
than that celebrated in *I*. 8. It would then be posssible to
place the changeover in 478 (Nicocles' among the first celery
crowns at the Isthmus) followed by his death between 478
and the composition of *I*. 8 in honour of Cleander after
Cleander's Isthmian victory in 476. It is certain that the
memory of Hellas' narrow escape from Xerxes and the anxieties of Pindar for Thebes will have been hardly less vivid in
476 than in 478. None of Finley's arguments for 478 in fact
rule out 476 as the date of *I*. 8. Pindar did not leave for Sicily
till after the Olympian games of that year, so that Finley's
fine words on the development of Pindar's calling, on the
relation between the close of *I*. 8 and the Sicilian odes, would
still hold. His general description indeeed is almost more
applicable to 476 than 478:

> It is not easy to conceive a more detailed or subtler commentary
> on the mixed bitterness and greatness of Greece in the years of
> the Persian invasion.[316]

Perspective has come and doubt and triumph mixed as the
months of actual combat recede. The Delian league in 478
and the broken unanimity of Sparta and Athens becloud the
horizon and might rightly be construed by the wise as 'flowers
of contention'.[317] 478 or 476 B.C., *I*. 8 gives us a terminus
ante quem for the changeover with a preference for 478 B.C.
for the changeover and 476 B.C. for the ode. The other odes
which refer to celery crowns are later: *O*. 13 locked in at 464
by the scholiast; *N*. 4 and *I*. 2 less securely dated – Bowra
gives *N*. 4 a queried 473 and *I*. 2 a queried 470.[318]

Corinthian celery. The symbolism of the change of crowns
was far reaching. It was meant to imply a whole-heartedly
Dorian and Peloponnesian stance by Corinth for the future,
an adherence to Dorian ways and the Dorian spirit, sometimes
obscured in the past by Corinth's vigorous and experimental

79

culture, her taste for the novel, the exotic, the imported. Who better to hymn this change in the context of the Isthmian agon than Pindar, a confirmed exponent of agonistic sacrality, of the hero's hold on eternity, of Heracles the Dorian as the archetypal hero?[319] It is in Pindar's four references to the celery crown that the significance of Corinth's changeover is disclosed.

Isthmian 2,[320] written circa 470 B.C. concerns Xenocrates of Acragas' victory in the chariot race.

...οὐκ ἄγνωτ᾽ ἀείδω
Ἰσθμίαν ἵπποισι νίκαν
Τὰν Ξενοκράτει Ποσειδάων ὀπάσαις
Δωρίων αὐτῷ στεφάνωμα κόμᾳ
πέμπεν ἀναδεῖσθαι σελίνων
εὐάρματον ἄνδρα γεραίρων, Ἀκραγαντίνων φάος.

I sing of the famous Isthmian victory which
Poseidon granted the horses of Xenocrates and
sent him a crown of Dorian celery wherewith
to bind his locks, honouring the charioteer,
the glory of the Acragantines.

We notice a contrast between the proclamation here of the stirring Dorian victory and the sordider *auri fames* excoriated in the first stanzas. This Dorian victory was won, Pindar proclaims, at the Isthmus and at the Isthmus now (as well as at Nemea) the crown of Dorian celery may be achieved.

Nemean 4,[321] written circa 473 B.C., makes the point even more strongly. The ode was written for the victory of Timasarchus of Aegina in the boys' wrestling, and wrestling, it will be remembered, with the pankration most vividly evoked the earlier spirit of the agon and Heracles' own struggles with man and beast.

Thy father would have rejoiced, Timasarchus,
and sung his victor son's circlet of crowns
from Cleonae's games and glorious renowned
Athens and seven-gated Thebes

— there is relatively little emphasis on Nemea, while in v. 85, speaking of Timasarchus' uncle Kallikles, Pindar tells how he

80

in the contest of Poseidon, the thunderer, the
Trident-bearer, won in youth's flower, the
flower of Corinth, celery.

...'Ορσοτριαίψα
ἵν' ἐν ἀγῶνι βαρυκτύπου
θάλησε Κορινθίοις σελίνοις·

Even though the ode is for a Nemean victory, the majesty
and dignity of Corinth's crown is stated more emphatically
than its Nemean original.

So too in *O*. 13.30,[322] written in 464 B.C. for Xenophon
of Corinth's double victory (stade and pentathlon) at Olympia.
The ode opens with the famous eulogy of Corinth itself ἐν τᾷ
γὰρ 'Εὐνομία ναίει (the same Eunomia Herodotus claimed
for Sparta as a peculiarly Dorian attribute) and extols the
singular combination of old and new, traditional and innovat-
ing that had distinguished Corinth in the past. Pindar then
turns to Xenophon's achievement: first the Olympic victory
in question, for Pindar could not diminish that, though there
is no reference to the olive by name ἀντεβόλησεν / τῶν ἀνὴρ
θνατὸς οὔπω τις πρότερον. Then straightaway the Isthmus:

Twin wreaths of celery crowned him at the Isthmus
also, and Nemea's voice concurred.

δύο δ' αὐτὸν ἔρεψαν
πλόκοι σελίνων ἐν 'Ισθμιάδεσσιν
φανέντα' Νέμεά τ' οὐκ ἀντιξοεῖ.

Later in the ode v. 49 comes a significant elevation of
Corinth's mythology: Sisyphus, Medea, and then Glaukos

before whom the Danaoi quaked in fear, to whom
he spoke with pride of his father's realm,
his palace and his rich apportionment away
in the city of Peirene.

Will sees in this reference an overt challenge to the Argive
claims to local hegemony:

et certes cette disposition irrédentiste s'explique
surtout par une hostilité violente à l'égard moins
des Proitides et des Atrides que de l'Argos historique.[323]

The 'exigences locales'[324] to which Pindar conforms are in fact one and the same with the motivation for the changeover of victors' crowns: the need to assert the authenticity of Corinth's role in the region, the true Dorian flavour, the legitimate προστασία of her fraternal states.

The failure of the response

In spite of Pindar, in spite of the celery crowns, in spite of the capture of Cleonae and the presidency of the Nemean games, Corinth failed in her political aims. She did not become a land power at the head of a loosely-grouped company of cities lying along the land isthmus which she dominated from Acrocorinth. She did not unite the corridor on the basis of traditional politics through the archaic modalities of agones and their myths. For this there were two reasons, one internal and domestic, the other external.

Internal factors. In the first place, the rulers of Corinth could not on this occasion manipulate their mythology for political ends any more than they had been able to in the past in the days of the Bacchiads and the Cypselids. The syncretistic ethos of the Isthmus was unshaken by the introduction of celery crowns and the proclamation of a new Dorian day. That same Xenophon, in whose honour Pindar wrote *O.* 13, dedicated for his victory in fulfilment of his vow a hundred temple prostitutes to the service of Cyprian Aphrodite, ματέρ' ἐρώτων οὐρανίαν, and persuaded a reluctant Pindar to commemorate this event also.[325] The likelihood of Corinthian culture becoming frozen in a pattern of nationalist propaganda was never more remote.

The life of the elder Laïs, insofar as it can be distinguished from her more celebrated namesake, attests the presence and the character of this rapidly growing cult.[326] Laïs, so legend went, was when a girl, visited by Aphrodite Melainis and claimed by the goddess as her servant: it was she who met Euripides ἐν κήπῳ τινὶ (Athenaeus, 582C): her career in Aphrodite's services was crowned by burial near the temple of Aphrodite Melainis which Pausanias passes within the Craneum grove: (the κῆπος perhaps of the Euripides' anecdote?). Aphrodite Melainis, Will suggests, is a chthonic divinity, blended with the figure of Ino, while Aphrodite Kypria is the adopted immigrant, anadyomene, associated with Cenchreae, with the nymph Leukothea, and of course with the harlot's profession. So that in Laïs both are mingled, a faithful reflection of the exploratory tendency of Corinth's religion at the time.

Moreover, the name Laïs has been thought to mean 'lioness', from the Semitic: Laïs' grave,[327] we note, was 'surmounted by a lioness holding a ram in her paws'. Will, in *Éléments orientaux dans la religion grecque ancienne*, has identified the significant elements of the cult of the Phrygian mother of the gods ('c'est d'abord une déesse au lion') as she was brought to Greece. He notes Pindar's references, from the 470's, and comments 'Mais où le poète avait-il rencontré la Phrygienne?'[328]

Might not the answer be, at Corinth, and at the Isthmus generally, for here there was a ready-made context for the Phrygian mother of the gods and her paredros Attis: the cult of a dead youth (Palaimon is not a child); a mother's threnody; and the pine branches, Attis' own symbol, which were already established in the cult of the drowned Palaimon,[329] the foundation of whose fifth-century temenos have only recently been uncovered? Attis and the Atthideia in Greece are usually dated to the late fifth century and then allowed only marginal significance. A recent analysis of the problem by N. Weill, however, has established 'qu' Adonis était connu et honoré à Athènes au milieu du Ve siècle'.[330] The mother of the gods herself, moreover, was no marginal figure in Pindar's dithyramb:

...σεμνᾷ μέν κατάρχει
ματέρι πὰρ μ[εγ]άλα ῥόμβοι τυπάνων,
ἐν δὲ κέχλαδ[εν] κρόταλ᾽, αἰθομένα τε
δᾷς ὑπὸ ξαν[θα]ῖσι πεύκαις.[331]

Before the great and mighty mother
ring tambourines, crash cymbals,
and the torch leaps glowing,
up to the tawny pines.

The tawny pines are, surely, pines illuminated by the glowing torch, if not themselves afire, and the dadophore may be none other than Attis himself.

Whether or not these suggestions: the spread of Kypria to the Isthmus, a syncretism with the Megala Mater, the fusion of Attis and Palaimon, prove well-founded or not, it is clear that the general character of Corinth's earlier cults persisted despite the post-480 reorganization. The attempt to Dorianize failed.

One instance of the persistence of archaic symbols is the continuation of the pine in cult after it had ceased to be the material of the victors' crowns. The cultic pine, as distinct from the agonistic victor's pine, continued in the celery period; that is, in the period between the introduction of the celery crown in ca. 478 B.C. and the reintroduction of the pine crown ca. 66 A.D. The evidence for this continuing presence of pine in cult may be reviewed:

(1) Musaeus said that there were two games at the Isthmus: one in honour of Poseidon, one in honour of Melikertes; and this comment Broneer dates to the fifth-fourth century. Elsewhere, e.g. Plutarch, *Theseus* 25.4, where two ceremonies are mentioned, that in honour of Melikertes is said to be a rite, τελετή, and in this rite, presumably, the pine played a part, so that Musaeus is some evidence for the cultic pine in the fifth century.[332]

(2) Euphorion in the third century knew of the pine in connection with the cult of Melikertes and distinguished this from its use in the early games, the one being the reason for the other. Euphorion is a good source, as noted, because of his specialist interest and comparatively close date.[333]

(3) Corinth IX, *Sculpture*, no. 55 has an interesting monument from Hellenistic times in which Cybele and her lion surmount a base, on the right side of which are represented Attis' ornaments: pine, pipe, and crook.[334]

(4) Statuary. A marble head purchased in Athens and presented to the Isthmian collection in April 1960 by Miss Polly Scribner Ames, would seem better classified as a satyr than a victor, and the pine crown thereon thus evidence of the continued cultic use of the pine. So too is the Stroganoff Zeus, a pine-wreathed Zeus which Cook connected with Attis on the strength of the pine crown, but could , as Dow says, equally well be associated with the Isthmian pine, or even, with both Attis and the Isthmian pine if, as has been suggested, the two tended to syncretize. The dates of these heads,

survivors, of course, of whole genres, probably precede the revival of the pine wreath.[335]

Thus the cultic pine did not disappear when the celery wreath came in as the victor's crown and eventually, as Plutarch says — and such epigraphic evidence as the Hatherton relief in the Metropolitan museum confirms — again became the victor's crown.[336] Therefore, from the vigorous continuity of the earlier Isthmian religion, the comparative failure of the policy of a change of crowns may be inferred: even so, the fact that once changed, the celery crown remained for some five centuries shows that the idea behind the change was not yot wholly anachronistic. The archaic pattern of politics has still some life in the 470's.

External factors. The external reason for the failure of Corinth's policies in 478 leads into the discussion of the new determinants of the politics of the northeast Peloponnese. Corinth in 478 could not reproduce the effect that Sparta's bones of Orestes policy had had on Tegea. The other states of the area did not alter course and adhere to Corinth merely because she now presided over the Nemean festival and had proclaimed a new, more Dorian style at the Isthmus. New determinants now affected political movement in the Peloponnese and spearheading the new movement was Themistocles, the most catalytic of all *novi homines* in Greek history.

Chapter V

ARGOS AND THE NEW POLITICS

The new politics at Athens

Just as sport, it has been argued, emerged as a separate and distinctive area of human activity in the fifth century, becoming then the autonomous and technical subject it has been since, so too, in unilinear development, politics separated itself out in the late sixth and early fifth centuries and became the professional and autarchic area of human life it has been in many — not all — parts of the world since. The ambience of the sacred was relinquished, the profane universe beckoned. Brelich's *Guerre, Agoni e Culti nella Grecia Arcaica* gives a comparable account of the emergence of warfare as an independent activity out of initiation contests, le contese rituali.[337]

The autonomy of politics is most clearly shown in its language and nowhere more strikingly than in the sudden appearance at this period of the same vocabulary of politics that still is the currency of political science:[338] μουναρχίη, ὀλιγαρχίη, δῆμος ἄρχων: monarchy, oligarchy, democracy, all three extant for the first time in Herodotus III, 80–82, the Debate of the Conspirators, a passage which there is no reason to suppose did not form part of Herodotus' first draft of the Persian history and may therefore have been written prior to 461 B.C.[339]

Moves had been made before Cleisthenes towards a purely political organization of society. For example, Bourriot's[340] study of the Athenian *genos* in the archaic period makes it probable that this institution, long suspected of being the

86

bearer of privilege, was in fact a symptom of the evolving polis, 'cité rudimentaire' as Glotz called it.[341] These had come to center insofar as they were articulated, round the concept *eunomia*, right distribution (Erasmus) juste repartition (Benveniste), to each his due, increasingly, of political privilege.[342] In *eunomia* (as in *isonomia* later), the ideas of justice and order interacted, thus the term came to be used of that society in which law and order obtain because a just repartition of privilege has been achieved. The Sparta of the Great *Rhetra*, Solonian Athens, post-Cypselid Corinth were all earlier or later designated *eunomiai* in this sense.[343] Yet all failed to perpetuate the secular mode of politics, for a variety of reasons. At Sparta, purely adventitious factors cut short the *antagoria* and *kratos* the assembly had gained at the expense of kings and elders. In Solon's Athens, the traditional structure of society was scarcely touched by his regrouping in τέλη. Post-Cypselid Corinth achieved a secular organisation and came close to anticipating the Cleisthenic transformation: yet once it is realized that not the fact of secularity alone but also a conceptualizing awareness of the process, plus a minimal duration of time are needed to establish the new order, Corinth's choice of the old tag *eunomia* betrays its weakness. Indeed it may be argued that *eunomia* (and all derivatives of νέμειν) hark back to one original function of the priest-king, viz. distribution, thus no eunomia was likely to be generative of new political categories.[344]

Cleisthenes' reform was 'un acte à la fois intellectuel et politique'.[345] This ambivalence, it could be said, is even reflected in the divergence of current research, accoridng to the emphasis placed on the reformer's political virtuosity or, alternatively, on the intellectual ascendancy over contemporaries embodied in his work. To the difference in emphasis corresponds a variation in perspective — the exegesis of *realpolitik* focussing an intense spotlight on a limited area, while *Ideengeschichte* not unnaturally plays its hazier searchlights over a wider range. *Coastal Demes of Attika* and *Clisthène L' Athénien*, two books current which are explicitly concerned with Cleisthenes, exemplify the contrast; yet it is not unfair to say that no appreciation which does not combine both aspects can be adequate.[346] An improved understanding of the distribution of the *demes* within the *trittyes*, a better grasp of the way sortition for the *provinciae* of the archons led on to κλήρωσις ἐκ προκρίτων, of the particular circumstances to meet which ostracism was introduced in 508/7 B.C., are as necessary but no more necessary than Ehrenberg's origins of democracy in polis religion and polis constitution, or the Lévêque — Vidal Naquet study of secular space and secular time, in the Cleisthenic calendar and *bouleuterion*. From Cleisthenes and from Themistocles (Cleisthenes' true successor) the historical conjuncture demanded intellectual stature no less than political ingenuity.[347]

The true measure of that stature is the half century of linguistic revolution which followed, as the idiom of politics underwent rapid and violent change. People ceased to inquire for example whether a regime measured up to some ancient ideal, some Golden Age, das gute alte Recht, instead the critical question became wer herrscht?, the identity of the ruling group, and, *pari passu* the cluster of words round *nomos* (*isonomia, eunomia, dysnomia, anomia*) gave way to -κρατία (or -αρχία) compounds, δημοκρατία, ἀριστοκρατία, ὀλιγαρχία. Meier in 'Drei Bemerkungen zur Vor- und Frühgeschichte des Begriffs Demokratie' analyses this change and describes it as 'die grosse Zäsur im Verfassungsdenken der Griechen'. The replacement of *thesmos* by *nomos* for the statutes of a community is hardly less important, pointing to the growth of a belief that only law self-imposed should be binding, not that which a lawgiver hands down. The changing sense of the prefix *iso* — (in *isegoria, isonomia, isomoiria*), the evolution of the pair δῆμος — πλῆϑος , the recession of the verbal element in compounds from the root -νεμ-: behind each of these lies a major political redefinition, behind the general restructuring of the *problematik* nothing less than a revolution in philosophy.[348]

The link between Cleisthenes and this transformation is not the doubtful hypothesis of ἰσονομία πολιτική as his (exclusive) slogan nor yet the vaguer consideration that his constitution is in fact the *terminus post quem* for all these experiments with language. Rather it lies in the scope and the consistency of his constitutional reform, in this visible evidence of abstract, anhistorical conceptualization, the only guarantee, arguably, of any real political understanding.

It is, moreover, only the practice of isolating political concepts from the accretions of history that enables these concepts to be used consciously and deliberately in the exchanges of everyday politics. So that here we have a possible answer to Ehrenberg's 'something of a puzzle how the aristocratic ἰσονομία could so quickly become the watchword of democracy'. Cleisthenes conceived of ἰσονομία unmarked, as the philologists say, the *parole* in contradistinction to the *langue*: the *eupatridai*, on the other hand, read into the word all their resentment of the tyrannis, of Hippias personally, of the failure at Leipsydrion (for there is also that other skolion, αἰαῖ Λειψύδριον, προδωσέταιρον). Cleisthenes understood the potential of ἰσονομία as the κάλλιστον ὄνομα of the hustings, understood too that the right word in the right song can have redoubled impact. There is no puzzle then in the adaptation: 'für Schlagworte gilt kein Urheberrecht' (Meier): only it was the measure of Cleisthenes' political skill that he had understood this.[349]

His legacy was an accelerating sophistication in the theory and practice of politics, in the operation as well as the definition of the formulae.

Between Cleisthenes and Themistocles there was an increasing radicalization of the political scene, the extension of democracy as both Kagan and Fornara characterize the eighties. The first use of ostracism in 488/7 B.C. (πρῶτος ὠστρακίσθη) being after all the point of Androtion F6 and *Ath. Pol.* 22, note also θαρροῦντος τοῦ δήμου in the latter) and the introduction of κλήρωσις ἐκ προκρίτων for the archons in 487/6 B.C., these set the stage for Themistocles' emergence on the scene in 483/2, more radical than Cleisthenes ever had been or ever could be.[350]

This radicalism of Themistocles consisted not so much in any extremism of dogma but rather in the overt and aggressive tenor of his public attitudes. He epitomized le défi athénien, he was, in Podlecki's striking phrase, the man who wielded the flail. Three examples from 483/477 B.C., Themistocles' heyday, illustrate what is meant.

There is, first, the conspicuous use of the demotic, Phrearrhios, on *ostraka* bearing Themistocles' name. Vanderpool explores the question How are we to explain the unusually large number of demotics? and concludes that Themistocles personally must have cultivated this form of address, that he wanted to be known as the Phrearrhian rather than as 'the son of Neocles'. There was no question of Themistocles concealing his patronymic and the obvious motive is that of principle, of public adherence to the new order.

Second, the epigram from the Piraeus wall,

ἀρξάμενοι πρῶτοι τειχίζειν οἵδ᾽ ἀνέθηκαν
βουλῆς καὶ δήμου δόγμασι πειθόμενοι

Jacoby is against all attempts to connect this inscription with Themistocles, the consecration by the entire college and the imitation of the epigram of Simonides are more in accord with a later date. After nearly a century however the imitation, if such it was, will have lost all pungency: immediately after Thermoplyae on the other hand, the contrast between *τοῖς κείνοις ῥήμασι* and *βουλῆς καὶ δήμου δόγμασι* will have been strident.

Finally, the tyrannicide statuary, the Kritios and Nesiotes group set up according, to the Parian Marble, in 477/6 B.C. It is not necessary to accept all Podlecki says of the anti-Alcmaeonid slant of the cult in order to follow him in associating the rededication of the group with Themistocles, nor is it obligatory to deny the earlier Antenor group any merit in order to prove that the more famous Harmodius and Aristogeiton statuary had a particular message for contemporaries — they were the archetypal republicans.[351]

But if radical, then proselytising: and what evidence is there that Themistocles made any effort to export the Athenian experiment? That Pericles would later encourage the replacement of oligarchies by democracies in the subject states of the Delian League, Erythrae and Samos for example, is common ground. Thucydides makes Phrynichus argue that the allies will be more loyal to a democracy in Athens than to an oligarchy, for with a democracy (scil. in Athens) the allied oligarchs are kept in check and the common people have a constant champion.[352] Greenidge has a fine passage on the result of the Delian League's first seventy years 478 —404 B.C.:

The effects of the empire were permanent. It had for seventy years fostered popular government in the East and inscriptions tell us with what result. The *βουλὴ καὶ δῆμος* appear as the governing power throughout the Aegean and in Asia Minor, at Samos, Chios, Paros, Mytilene, Halicarnassus, Rhodes, Byzantium, and many other cities. Crushed for a moment by Spartan despotism, many of these cities again sought Athens as a liberator and to assert their freedom formed the alliance generally known as the Second Athenian Confederacy.[353]

But can Themistocles be implicated in this development, usually considered to date only from the mid-fifties of the fifth century? Apart from the case of Argos to be considered below, the accusation of Themistocles' contemporary, Timocreon of Rhodes, quoted by Plutarch, bears on the argument:

τοὺς μὲν κατάγων ἀδίκως, τοὺς δ' ἐκδιώκων, τοὺς δὲ καίνων.

Some he restored to power, others he banished, and others again
he put to death.

The reference is to an expedition made by Themistocles around the Aegean after Salamis, during which a careful selection of exiles was restored, Timocreon of Ialysos in Rhodes, a member of an oligarchic élite, being among the unlucky candidates for restoration, hence the accusation of bribery. The language, κατάγων ἐκδιώκων, is suggestive of political changes, not merely personal vicissitudes, and Themistocles may in fact have been installing a series of popular regimes up and down the islands subverting the legal order, as Timocreon's use of the term ἀδίκως would naturally imply.[354]

Themistocles and Argos

This proselytising fervour, it is argued, prompted the ostracized Themistocles to mastermind the transformation of Argos from oligarchy to democracy. The date of this change cannot be certainly established. The caretaker government has been taken as oligarchic, despite the arguments on the other side for its democratic character. This caretaker government was demoted and expelled when the sons of those who were slain by Cleomenes grew up.[355] ἐπηβήσαν is Herodotus' word, became ephebes, which at Athens meant 18 and this points to a date in the early seventies for the recovery of the upper hand in the state by the sons of the fallen: even those born

91

posthumously to the slain at Sepeia would be 18 in 476 B.C. and these will have been only a small percentage. 478 is a more likely date overall.

In an important reappraisal, Forrest collected evidence for the state of Argive internal politics in the seventies and sixties. He noted for example that already in 479 B.C. Themistocles protected Argos from reprisals for her Medism because he hoped or knew that the Argive leaders at the time would be prepared to join a democratic anti-Spartan alliance. He also cited the Argive dedication at Delphi of a group of statues of the *Epigonoi*, the original *Epigonoi* that is, who succeeded where their fathers failed in capturing Thebes, a natural choice of subject, he suggested, for the fifth century *Epigonoi* when they recovered control of Argos from the interim government. This dedication Forrest dated 470–465 B.C. Finally, Forrest considered Pindar's tenth *Nemean*, for Theaeus the Argive, as possible evidence for an oligarchic government back in power at Argos in the early 460's. Forrest put the evidence together, added his original case for a democratic *coup* after Sepeia in 494, and arrived at a complicated scheme as follows (1) a democratic government of the *douloi* down to c. 468 B.C.; (2) recovery of power by the sons of the slain in 468 B.C. (flight of Themistocles, base at Delphi, Theaeus ode); (3) ejection of the sons of the slain in 464 B.C. (Aeschylus' account of Argive democracy in the *Suppliants*, vv. 605–624, which was first performed in 463 B.C.).[356]

But this entire scheme rests on a misunderstanding of what Aristotle said in Book Five of the *Politics*, which was that the chance loss of life on any scale by the richer section of the community, the nobility, tended to favour the development of democracy. The paragraph may be pressed to provide three *progressively more gradual* examples of this happening: (1) a sudden and definite transfer of power, as at Tarentum; (2) some change in the balance of power, as Argos; (3) a long-drawn-out and never-explicit drift towards ochlocracy, as at Athens in the Peloponnesian war. Argos thus illustrates a mean between two extremes: it was an explicitly democratic change but also took place over a period of time.[357] This would point to the acceptance by the sons of the slain *themselves* of the necessity of turning democratic in the face of the numerical weakness of their group after the recovery of power, a recognition that the rank and file had to be conciliated by the grant of a democratic constitution. Forrest himself seems to see the advantages in this interpretation of events when he suggests that (in 464) the sons of the slain may as well have undergone a change of heart as been expelled (lost control or changed their minds): and thus we may avoid positing either counter-revolution (468) or revolutionary coup at Argos (464) when there is such sketchy evidence for both.[358] After Sepeia, then, the only change which occurred, it is argued, was the (peaceful) recovery of power from the caretaker régime by the sons of the slain, to be dated in the early 470's.

Constitutional development towards democracy, however, on the part of the sons of the slain *themselves* (influenced by Themistocles) is a probability for the late 470's. Having won Argive goodwill by his protection of their city in 479 B.C., Themistocles, fleeing from Athens in 472 B.C. was the ideal mentor for an Argos intending to turn itself into a democracy. The origins of Argive democracy and Themistocles' stay in Argos have long been loosely associated: 'Zuerst bemühte sich Themistokles um das argivisch-athenische Bündnis...Vielleicht erst als Bundesgenossen der Athener bildeten die Argeien ihre Verfassung zur Demokratie aus.'[359] Yet for those who do not with Forrest see the *douloi* of Herodotus as democrats in disguise, the advent of democracy is usually dated later, to the period when the treaty came into force after Kimon's fall, in 461 B.C.[360] In view of the fact that Themistocles' name is associated with the other democratic developments of the region, namely, the synoecism and democracy of, in turn, Elis, Mantinea, and Tegea, all of which, it is suggested, he initiated from a base in Argos, would it not be more plausible to associate him directly with the change in Argos itself, the prerequisite, surely, for the remainder of his radical activities?

The redating of Aeschylus' *Suppliants* to 463 B.C.[361] is evidence for democracy in Argos before the Argive-Athens treaty and indeed Aeschylus' evidence suggests democratic institutions contemporary with Themistocles' sojourn there, if that is allowed to be the political reference of the play. Podlecki insists on the constitutional reference of such phrases as δήμου δεδόκται παντελῆ ψηφίσματα and δήμου κρατοῦσα χείρ which he characterizes as slogans in his summing up.[362] Others, however, have thought the reference to be not to Argos but to Athens itself, as the 490's dating seemed to indicate. This was Ehrenberg's interpretation, but it is made less plausible now that a date for the play in the late 460's has won general acceptance. The analysis of the *Suppliants* in the light of the revised dating agrees better with the concept of an Argive democracy, inspired by Themistocles, and later on his grateful protector for as long as possible; a political posture the playwright commends in a tribute to Argos some six years after the events concerned.

It is significant that the two developments of the eighties in Athens, the vigorous application of ostracism and the incipient rise of an effective executive in the *strategia* recur in Argos under the democratic régime: οἷον ἐν ῎Αργει καὶ ᾿Αθήνησιν says Aristotle of ostracism, showing thereby that the institution came to be associated with the former *polis* also. The central executive at Argos was the board of five generals and this prominence would gain in siginificance if the suggestion of a στρατηγία at Athens for Themistocles in 483/2 B.C. were accepted, for that would make him the first to exploit the possibilities (αὐτοσχεδιάζειν τὰ δέοντα) of the consistent (if affluent) mediocrity of the archontate and the concomitant rise of the *strategoi*.[363]

More than this; as Diamantopoulos has pointed out, the evidence of the *Suppliants* suggests that the spirit of the new politics, a general revision of the political and religious character of authority,[364] which is the theme of Athenian political life in the first half of the fifth century, was as present in Argos as in its original home, Athens. Among the central motifs of the *Suppliants* for example, is the insistence of the king (Pelasgos) that his authority and all authority in the state derives from the demos itself and this subordination is declared inherent in the royal estate, whether divinely sanctioned or as established by the bonds of clan and kin.[365] This must indicate a familiarity among the Argives not only with the letter but the spirit of radical democratic politics at least by 463 B.C., when the play was produced, and probably earlier, in the period to which the play refers, namely the years of Themistocles' exile in Argos.

It is now possible to turn from the internal politics of Argos in the 470's to her external situation, and consider the implications for Argive foreign policy of the constitutional transformation brought about by the sons of the slain under the guidance of Themistocles.

Argive external affairs

A date ca. 476 for the restoration of the *Epigonoi* and a date ca. 471 for Themistocles' arrival and a change to democracy by the 'sons of the slain' have been argued. What were the external circumstances of Argos at this period?

They were not at all promising: 'hated of all thy neighbours' seems still to have been an apt characterization of the Argive situation in the mid 470's.[366] Her pro-Mede neutralism had exposed her to threats of retaliation after Plataea, while Mycenae and Tiryns had felt able to assert an independence of their diminished hegemon by sending their own contingents to the Persian wars. The preceding chapter showed how Corinth had seized the opportunity to take over the Temenid heritage by usurping the presidency of the Nemean games and then inaugurating a change of crowns at the Isthmian games to consolidate a new Dorian stance. The new rulers of Argos, the Epigonoi, thus confronted a major challenge to Argos' status as a significant power in the northeast Peloponnese. They will have needed badly allies and policies: thus, they did not prevent the now-superannuated caretaker government from taking and holding Tiryns nor the Mycenaeans from challenging their leadership in the Argolid itself.[367] Until 471 B.C., when Themistocles arrived in Argos, they had only the hint of support given by his anti-reprisals policy in 479 B.C. When he arrived, however, the new Argos was born, a new constitution created, a new mode of foreign policies begun. The northeast Peloponnese was to be united and to confront Corinth on the one hand and Sparta on the other with a new strength won from progressive and revitalizing political ideology in contrast with the older unities of myth and cult. Or so it was hoped.

Synoecism and democracy in Elis, Mantinea and Tegea

Elis. Diodorus places the synoecism of Elis in 471/0 B.C. and it is significant that his brief notice of this event is followed

95

at once by a long account of Spartan hostility to Themistocles and his ultimate expulsion from the Peloponnese.[368] Strabo says that the synoecism of Elis, like that of Mantinea, was brought about by the Argives.[369] As to democracy in Elis, a series of Elean inscriptions shows it to have been closely modelled on the Athenian prototype: references to a βουλή of 500 and a δῆμος πληθύων among the early inscriptions are striking in this regard.[370] Democratic Elis, like Athens and Argos, seems to have kept the title of king, *basileus*, for one of its chief magistrates. On the other hand, as at Mantinea, at least some of the other magistrates were called *demiourgoi* (public servants), a title less likely to derive from a former organization by demes than to be included as an assertion of the strength of the new concept of popular sovereignty in both communities. The date of the synoecism of Elis, the involvement of Themistocles and his Argive patrons, together with the character of Elean democracy as seen in the epigraphic evidence, if put together, supply the first indication of newly democratised Argos' Peloponnesian diplomacy.

Mantinea. The evidence for Mantinea is less precise. Andrewes writes:

> We can probably associate with this (the synoikism of Elis) the founding of the city of Mantineia and the establishment of democratic constitutions in both states

and later 'the late 470's are an entirely likely period', scil. for the συνοικισμός.[371] The plausible step from a synoecism to a democracy is also made by Bölte: 'Es liegt nahe, aus dem Synoikismos einen Übergang zur Demokratie zu erschliessen.[372]' It is true that the revival of Spartan authority in Mantinea brought διοικισμός and oligarchy with it; the reverse, an implied association of Argive influence, synoecism and democratic change of constitution in Mantinea in the 470's rests only on its own plausibility: not even an Apollodorus date is available in support.[373] Andrewes' argument that Themistocles must have been engaged in subversion of this kind or the Spartans would not have insisted on his expulsion shows in what short supply hard evidence is.[374]

Tegea. So also, unfortunately, with Tegea. The synoecism is mentioned by Strabo in the same sentence as that of Mantinea, and Elis is dealt with in the same passage: perhaps, then, all three events were close in time.[375] Also, it is possible, as Forrest says, that Strabo is stating that the Argives synoecized Tegea as well as Mantinea, i.e. that ὑπ' Ἀργείων is to be understood with the second clause as well.[376] Polyaenus supplies the information that Tegea was a democracy by the 460's, if the context of chapter ten of Book Two is allowed to imply the total discomfiture of the laconizing faction in that city.[377]

One point may be made in this connection as to the effect on relations between Tegea and Mantinea of the new politics: the unversalist mode of politics superseding the older particularist directions derived from archaic religion, had every chance of overriding the persistent, traditional opposition of the two communities. It is not therefore necessary to argue, as Andrewes does, that it was because Mantinea turned democratic that Tegea adopted the opposite course. Secular politics emancipated city states from the ties and feuds of the former culture and obliterated the patterns of the archaic age. Insofar as the hostility of Tegea and Mantinea had its roots in cultural disagreements, these would be set aside when both became democratic. Insofar, however, as they were merely a product of rivalry for the water meadows on middle ground between the two, they persisted.

Is this series of probabilities the best that can be done with the evidence for the synoecism and democracy of Elis, Mantinea, and Tegea? Fortunately, supplementary material is available from Arcadian coin issues and has recently been reanalysed by Roderick T. Williams in *The Confederate Coinage of the Arcadians in the Fifth Century B.C.*[378] Following Hiller von Gaertringen, Williams suggests a synoecism for Mantinea and Tegea as early as ca. 477, and associates the opening of a new Arcadian mint at each of these two cities with the foundation of the new communities.[379] He goes on to isolate a 'second period' in this (numismatic) phase which is marked, on his analysis, by a sudden

period of intense activity marked by a complex crossing of dies, use of dies long after the appearance of flaws, a reduction of weight in the Tegea and Mantinea mints, and an experiment with fixed dies in the Mantinea mint.

In other words, there was an atmosphere of crisis which Williams associates with the battle of Tegea.[380] To the beginning of this period of intense activity Williams gives an upper date ca. 475 and a lower terminus of ca. 473 B.C. Thus he separates (in effect) the synoecism (opening of the new mints) from the change from oligarchy to democracy (period of intense activity) and supposes a 2 year gap between the two. He also argues, and plausibly, that the fact that all three mints (Cleitor, Tegea and Mantinea) experienced parallel developments in the period goes some way to establish a united Arcadian front at this time.[381] At the least, what the mints signify is a heightening throughout the 470's of the political temperature in the southern Arcadian cities, as Pausanias was disgraced and Sparta's influence waned, paralleled at Argos by the recovery of power on the part of the sons of the slain as they saw an era of opportunity open in the central Peloponnese. Williams' analysis of the coinage focuses attention on political developments in Arcadia in the early and middle seventies: at best, it can be associated with the picture of a restless Arcadia and Argos being brought to fever pitch by Themistocles, under whose aegis both synoecism and democracy spread throughout the area, a solid anti-Spartan bloc across the northern Peloponnese.[382]

This transformation took time and occupied the whole of Themistocles' stay at Argos, here dated 471—469 B.C. But for Argos the new politics seem to have borne immediate fruit: Corinth's grip on Nemea was destroyed. The dedication by the Argives at Olympia of spoils won from Corinthians[383] may well refer to the recovery of Nemea and the liberation of Cleonae from Corinth, which was found fighting at Argos' side during the siege of Mycenae in 468 B.C. Further, when challenging Argos for the hegemony of the Argolid, Mycenae, so Diodorus says, had laid claim to the Argive Heraion and to the direction of the Nemean games: ἠμφισβητοῦν δὲ καὶ περὶ τῶν ἱερῶν τῆς Ἡρὰς καὶ τὸν ἀγῶνα τῶν Νεμέων ἠξιοῦν αὐτοὶ διοικεῖν.[384] But if, in the late 70's, Corinth were still in control of the Nemean games, there would be little point in Mycenae challenging Argos for them. We may therefore reason that Argos had been successful in reasserting her claims by the closing years of the decade. Elis also, away on the other side of the Peloponnese, found that synoecism and democracy provided the necessary strength for an impressive extension of territory southward into Triphylia. The mints of Arcadia — Cleitor, Tegea, and Mantinea — synchronized their output as never before and for the whole alliance, in 470/69, the chances of a successful victorious decade ahead must have seemed excellent.

Break-up of the alliance. In the event, however, neither victory nor even permanence crowned the alliance. The first blow to fall was Themistocles' flight from Argos to the west, to Corcyra and Epirus, en route for Persia. Forrest, who dates this event to 469/8 B.C., is

> fairly certain that the collapse of democracy in Argos and the flight of Themistocles are in some way closely linked with each other.[385]

While agreeing with Forrest's date, it is possible to disagree with his interpretation of the political setting. It is not necessary to hypothesize counterrevolution in Argos to account for Themistocles' flight, for he was not expelled, nor threatened with expulsion, but made the decision freely when he heard ($\pi\rho o\alpha\iota\sigma\vartheta\acute{\alpha}\mu\epsilon\nu o\varsigma$) of the impending trial on which the Spartans were resolved.[386] He left his money with friends in Argos and five years later was able to recover it from them. Aeschylus' presentation of the *Suppliants* and propaganda in the *Oresteia* trilogy loses its political relevance if Themistocles chose to flee because he was certain the Argives could not or would not protect him. 'The Argive folk, faithful and ever true' would seem curious praise if there had been any possibility of extradition for Themistocles! It is more probable that he saw, not so much danger, as no future for himself in the Peloponnese, once Sparta was roused against him. He preferred to seek new fields of activity either to the west or east of mainland Greece. His going, however, weakened the alliance of democratic states with Argos at their head. Themistocles might have been able to prevent the distortion of political vision that followed, to persuade Mantinea to stay with the alliance, to deter Argos from pursuing chauvinist ends and so fragmenting the group effort, to keep alive the animating, proselytizing purpose that had given the alignment such a good start.[387]

With Themistocles gone, the Arcadian-Argive alliance was

faced with hostilities on two fronts. Within the Argolid, animosity between Mycenae and Argos flared into open war, and the Argives, in company with the Cleonaeans and Tegeates, laid siege to the ancient stronghold in 468/7. Outside the Argolid at the southern terminus of the highway, the Argives and the Tegeates took on the Spartan army and were defeated at the battle of Tegea.[388] If a proportion of Tegeate and Argive troops were away from the battlefield of Tegea, detained at the siege of Mycenae, the defeat of the alliance on the field would have been a foregone conclusion. Thus Argos' failure to synoecize the Argolid earlier was expensive: the disaffection of Tiryns later in the decade had its roots in the same error of judgment, based fundamentally, it may be noted, on the exclusive character of Argive culture so often demonstrated in the archaic period and, in spite of Themistocles and democracy, not yet fully eradicated.

Defeat at Tegea dampened the zeal of the allies not only for each other, but for the new style of politics that held them together. Mantinea now lost its democracy or at least its enthusiasm[389] and reverted to a pro-Sparta, anti-Tegeate policy, deserting the Arcadian line of battle at Dipaea in 466 B.C. and coining money for the Lacedaemonian pay-packets just before the battle.[390] Argos itself seems to have regressed at different levels to her prerevolutionary pattern. For example, a coin from Tegea in the first section of Williams' Period III (468–460 B.C.) featuring Zeus Meilichios, suggests that this cult, common to Tegea and Argos, was being stressed in the area as the basis for cooperative effort, rather than, for example, the shared commitment to a particular form of government.[391] Argos seems to have turned away from the larger issues and problems of the Peloponnese and to have concentrated solely on the reduction of Mycenae, and may even not have been present at Dipaea where Sparta defeated all the Arcadians but the Mantineans, Tisamenus' third victory. When Mycenae finally succumbed in 464, it appears that even the Cleonaeans no longer retained the enthusiasm for Argive hegemony, for Pausanias says that some of the refugees from Mycenae took refuge at Cleonae.[392]

One other episode may be relevant to this account of the disintegrating coalition, namely Pindar's sixth Olympian, which Wilamowitz argued, was intended to appease the Spartans and reconcile them with the Arcadians of

Stymphalia.[393] The poem is dated 468/7 by Wilamowitz, and may therefore be yet another instance of Arcadian defection at this time.

The change in the political climate of the northeast Peloponnese is to be accounted for by the evaporation, on Themistocles' departure, of confidence in the new 'professional' politics after the Athenian model and the reversion on the part of all concerned to foreign policies reminiscent of the archaic conventions. For example, the Phigaleian agitator at Tiryns is described as a seer, while in the tenth Nemean Ode, Pindar contends that it is the amalgam of mythical genealogies which binds the Argolid together.[394]

The Argive attempt to unite this area on the basis of the new politics of class and party failed as conclusively as had Corinth's attempt to rally the corridor communities round a system based on the old politics of shrines and games.

The reasons for Argive failure

As with Corinth, the reasons for Argos' failure to build a unified northeast Peloponnese on the basis not of culture but of politics stemmed from two sources, one external, one internal.

External factors. Mycenae's challenge to Argive hegemony has been seen to rest on the claim to ownership of the Heraeum a few miles to the southeast, and to the presidency of the Nemean games: both signs of a traditional approach to politics and evidence that Mycenae at least would not be easily won over to democratic solidarity. Tiryns also, roused to revolt by a Phigaleian 'seer' (*mantis*) seems tied to the former political mode.

Beyond the Argolid, in Arcadia also there is evidence that the traditional culture had not yet lost its hold on political developments. As Macan observes with reference to the rising at Tiryns,

This Arkadian diviner is one of a class of adventurers, other specimens of which are seen in Tisamenos of Elis [Hdt.] 9.33, Hegistratos 9.37, Antichares of Eleon 5.43, Kallias 5.44.[395]

101

It was the early sixth century which saw these seers and shamans in their heyday: characteristic then of Arcadia (possibly of Phigaleia in particular) to cling to the earlier rather than the later archaic political styles.[396]

Even where, as in the lower-lying civic communities of Mantinea and Tegea, Themistocles and his Argive associates could push through synoecism and democratic reform, still there remained enough of the older tradition of Arcadia to give rise to some doubt as to the true inspiration of the phenomena. Is it not possible that the institution of the Common Hearth of the Arcadians both at Tegea and Mantinea belongs to this period and may indicate a more traditionalist approach to the unification of outlying settlements than fifth century rationalism would altogether approve?[397] In these two cases the Common Hearth does not seem to have taken the usual form of a perpetual flame, kept alight in the *Prytaneion*. In Mantinea, at least, it was simply the round tomb of Antinoë; in Tegea, it is not clear what type of building is meant. The Mantinean tomb seems to have served as a shrine to inaugurate the synoecism and to have been known thereafter as the Common Hearth: Antinoë, the mythical synoecist of Mantinea, divinely inspired by a serpent, would be an appropriate patroness of the fifth century synoecism, represented as the refoundation of her work.[398] Thus the Mantineans at least may have achieved their synoecism in 470 B.C. in an altogether archaic spirit, making of it a sacred rite or repetition of *illud tempus*, an act contrary in spirit to the new profane politics of Cleisthenian Athens.

Internal factors. Even the Argives themselves seem not entirely liberated from the cultural prejudices of the archaic era. For evidence, Aeschylus' *Suppliants* is again crucial. In *JHS* 1957, Diamantopoulos analyses carefully the Argive attitudes depicted by the poet in the tragedy.[399] His conclusion is that the Argives, even in their adherence to democratic institutions, maintained that obsessive antiquarianism and emphasis on genealogical legend that the earlier cultural survey of Argos exhibited so markedly. The Danaid Trilogy seems to have been organised round the dynastic descent of the kings of Argos: from Io to the Danaids in the *Suppliants*; from Hypermnestra to Heracles in the *Danaids*; the reference of the *Egyptians* is no longer recoverable. In the *Suppliants* the Argive king Pelasgos, whom we have seen affirming the supremacy of the secular state, is also made to set out in detail the minutiae of his own birth and descent.[400]

He is the son of earth-born Palaichthon, he rules over the whole Peloponnese and mainland Greece as far as Strymon and Dodona. In this way the spectators are reminded not only of the seniority of the Argive dynasty over that of Sparta, but also of the seniority of Argos as a political power ruling over Greece.[401]

Diamantopoulos goes on to point out that this emphasis is Argos', not Aeschylus' own, since in the *Oresteia* the poet changes his tune to stress Athens' supremacy, though in less protracted terms. Even the demos in the *Suppliants* is portrayed as preoccupied with its own antiquity: nine generations before Heracles as opposed to an alternative tradition dating democracy back to six generations before the hero. Diamantopoulos comments:

The discrepancy of the Argive tradition as to the time when the demos took over authority may be explained thus: in its struggle for power the demos wished to be associated with the earliest and most glorious pages of Argive history in order to acquire weighty historical titles showing that the democratic constitution was ancestral.[402]

This is not the attitude of a community which has taken to heart the message of a political revolution, of the need for transformation from a hieratic obscurantist world order to a new self-validating domain of secular politics. With so imperfect a hold on the ideological basis for union, Argos was not surprisingly unable to make the new politics a viable cohesive force whereby the northeast Peloponnese might be rallied round one of its cardinal foci and welded into a significant political unit.

POSTFACE

The first chapter of this essay described the region with whose vicissitudes in the crucial years 480–460 B.C. the narrative has been concerned. The existence of an axial corridor, the alignment of communities along it, the strategic and logistic capabilities of the zone were there outlined. But as Febvre in founding the school of historical geography reiterates: 'Des nécessités nulle part. Des possibilités, partout', and man himself and his own nature determine the utilization of these possibilities.[403] The second chapter therefore outlined the cultural background of the region in its widest sense, the archaic world of the northeast Peloponnese, the orientation generations of settlement had given to society in the area. The differences, counterproductive of union, outweighed in the archaic period (that is, to the end of the sixth century) any centripetal movement. For archaic politics rested on archaic religion, *was* archaic religion, and in this sphere, Corinth, Argos, and Arcadia exhibited marked differences. Among the determinants of archaic politics, the crown games stood out by reason of their origin in the archaic period and their expression of the spirit of that period (Chapter 3). In the fifth century, the incipient change from archaic to classical politics, from a sacred to a profane *Weltanschauung* made itself felt: a transitional period, therefore, in which first Corinth (Chapter 4) and next Argos (Chapter 5) tried first the former modalities (Chapter 4) and then the new style of political adventure (Chapter 5). Both failed to achieve the union of the region thereby and yet the possibility for union, less through the old determinants, more through the new, continued to exist. In this connection the episode of 392 B.C. when Corinth and Argos were briefly merged on the basis of democratic politics acquires added interest.[404]

104

Yet it must not be forgotten that even the possibilities alter.

Tout acte modifie à la fois l'agent et le milieu: les états d'équilibre se détruisent incessamment par leur propre jeu et font place à de nouveaux équilibres. Le facteur temps revêt ainsi son importance.[405]

With the extra Peloponnesian activities of Sparta (whose importance Busolt alone underlines) the eclipse of the northeast Peloponnese as an autonomous and viable zone begins. The fifth century with Sparta's repeated excursions across the Isthmus of Corinth saw the process accelerate until in the early fourth century, it is even doubtful whether a united Corinth or Argos, had it lasted, could have significantly affected the regional distribution of power in Greece. But in the period 480–460 B.C., with which this essay has been concerned, the projected union, on whatever basis, was never given the opportunity.

NOTES

1. For the French school of human geography, whose *possibiliste* ideas have shaped this chapter, see principally Lucien Febvre, *La Terre et l'Évolution humaine* (Paris, 1922), Max. Sorre, *L'Homme sur la Terre* (Paris, 1961), and P. Claval, "Géographie et Profondeur Sociale", *Annales, Économies, Sociétés, Civilisations*, 22.5 (September-October 1967) 1005-1046. The following quotations have been particularly formative: Le vrai, le seul problème géographique, c'est celui de l'utilisation des possibilités (Febvre, 425) and Il y a une dialectique incessante entre l'homme qui façonne le payage, qui l'humanise et le paysage (avec la nature de son sol, son régime climatique) qui limite le choix de la raison, R. Bastide, Y a-t-il une crise de la psychologie de peubles? *Revue de Psychologie des Peuples* 21 (1966) 8-20 cited by Claval, 1012. See also Y. Chataigneau and J. Sion, Pays Balkaniques in P. Vidal de la Blache and L. Gallois, eds., *Géographie Universelle* (Paris, 1934) VII.II, ch. 36, for a geography of Greece by this school, and E. Will, *Korinthiaka, Recherches sur l'histoire et la Civilisation de Corinthe des Origines aux Guerres Médiques* (Paris, 1955), who also invokes Max. Sorre for his opening chapter.

2. Strabo, *Geography* 8.6.5.; A. Philippson, *Die Griechischen Landschaften* (Frankfurt, 1959) III.I, 93. *PWK* col. 787, s.v. Argos; Pausanias, *Description of Greece*, Book II.

3. Fernand Braudel, *La Méditerranée et le Monde méditerranéen a l'époque de Philippe II* (Paris, 1949), 144, quatre fuseaux d'histoire. Braudel's characterization of four north-south isthmi across Europe provokes several parallels.

4. For Corinth, see Strabo 8.6.20-23; Pausanias 2.1.1 − 2.5.4; J. G. Frazer, *Pausanias's Description of Greece* (New York, 1965), III, 1-39; G. Roux, *Pausanias en Corinthie* (Paris, 1958), 105-130; E. Kirsten and W. Kraiker, *Griechenlandkunde* (Heidelberg, 1967), I, 312-329; *Corinth, Results of the excavations conducted by the American School of Classical Studies at Athens*, I, I; H. N. Fowler and R. Stilwell, *Introduction, Topography, Architecture* (Cambridge, Mass. 1932); R. Carpenter and A. W. Parsons, *The Defenses of Acrocorinth and the Lower Town* (Cambridge, Mass., 1936) III, II; C. Broneer, *The Odeum* (Cambridge, Mass., 1932) X; *PWK* cols. 991-1036 s.v. Korinthos.

5. A. Phillippson, *Die Griechischen Landschaften* (Frankfurt, 1959) III.I, 86.

6. For Acrocorinth in the S. E., see Corinth III.I, 43; and in general J. Wiseman, *Land of the Ancient Corinthians* (Göteborg, 1978) and M. Sakellariou and N. Faraklas, *Corinthia and Cleonae* (Athens, 1971). W. Kendrick Pritchett in *Studies in Ancient Greek Topography*, III discusses the travellers' approach via the Phliasian Gate.

7. For Tenea, see Strabo 8.6.22; Pausanias 2.5.3, P. Levi, *Pausanias: Guide to Greece* (London, 1971) I, 143 n. 34; W. Leake, *Travels in the Morea* (Amsterdam, 1968) III, 320.

8. Corinth III.I, 96; Frazer III, 85-89; *British Naval Intelligence Handbook to Greece* (London, 1945) 167.

9. Strabo 8.6.22.

10. For Cleonae, see Strabo 8.6.19; Pausanias 2.15.1-2; Leake III, 325; Frazer III, 82-88; Philippson III.I, 92; Roux, 171.

11. Philippson III.I, 92.

12. Leake III, 115. The *difficulty* of an approach over the mountains, as distinct from the existence of such a route, is underestimated by Pritchett, 13 and 33-35.

13. Frazer III, 87.

14. Lucian, *Charon* 23.

15. For Nemea, see Strabo 8.6.19; Pausanias 2.15.2; Leake III, 330-337; C. W. Blegen, The American Excavation at Nemea, Season of 1924 *Art and Archaeology* 19 (1925) 175-184 and Excavations at Nemea, 1926 *AJA* 31 (1927) 421-440. For later reports see below N.305. Pritchett III, 244 discusses the possibility of Nemea's having been a station on the *cursus publicus* as shown on the Peutinger Table. It is, incidentally, noticeable that the Table shows (in effect) only the one arterial route in the NE Peloponnese.

16. Pindar, *N.* 6.45.

17. Thucydides 5.58-60; Pritchett II, 98-99. See also A. Andrewes and K. J. Dover, *A Historical Commentary on Thucydides* (Oxford, 1970) IV, 78-84.

18. For Phlius, see Strabo 8.6.24; Pausansias 2.12.3 − 2.13.6; Leake III, 339-345; A. G. Russell, The Topography of Phlius and the Phliasian Plain, *Annals of Archaeology and Anthropology* 11 (1924) 37-47.

19. E. Meyer, *Peloponnesische Wanderungen* (Zurich, 1939) 18.

20. Frazer IV, 230.

21. Philippson III.I, 201.

22. *British Naval Intelligence. Handbook to Greece*, III, 173; Busolt, *Die Lakedaimonier und Ihre Bundesgenossen* (Leipzig, 1878) 229; Pritchett II, 80 (where surely γῆν rather than ὁδὸν understood with ἀμφίαλον would solve the problem?). Pritchett III, ch. 5 is itself an excellent evaluation of the problems set by ancient thoroughfares, let alone byways.

23. Frazer III, 215; IV, 194; see, however, Pritchett III, ch. 1 who with Philippson identifies this pass as Prinus, putting the Climax pass in the Tourniki area to the south.

24. Roux, 156; cf. Meyer, 11.

25. For Mycenae, see Strabo 8.6.19; Pausanias 2.15.4 − 2.16.4; Frazer III, 94-164. Chataigneau-Sion, 551 writes Mycènes, à l'entrée des défilés, dans un décor vraiment tragique.

26. Diodorus 11.65.2.

27. See E. Vermeule, *Greece in the Bronze Age* (Chicago, 1964) 118 for traces of Mycenaean roads.

28. On Bronze Age Corinth see Will, 26; on Athens, see O. Broneer, "Athens in the Late Bronze Age" *Antiquity* 30 (1956) 9-19; on Sparta, J. T. Hooker, *The Ancient Spartans* (London, 1980), 32-41.

29. On Argos, see Strabo 8.6.7-8.6.11; Pausanias 2.18.1-2.24.8; Leake I, 394-411; R. A. Tomlinson, *Argos and the Argolid* (London, 1972).

30. Philippson III.I, 142.

31. Chataigneau-Sion, 551.

32. Vermeule, 30.

33. Frazer III, 234.

34. Chataigneau-Sion, 550.

35. F. Gschnitzer, *Abhängige Orte im Griechischen Altertum* (Munich, 1958) 81.

36. On Tegea, see Strabo 8.8.2; Pausanias 8.44.8-8.54.5; Philippson III.I, 257.

37. Plutarch, *Lycurgus*. On Spartan austerity see A. J. Holladay, "Spartan Austerity" *CQ* 27 (1977) 111-126; P. Cartledge, *Sparta and Lakonia* (London, 1979) 154-157.

38. On Mantinea, see Strabo 8.8.2; Pausanias 8.8.3-8.9.5; Leake I, 101-109; III, 97-98.

39. See note 23 above.

40. Few roads could carry wheeled traffic — those that could were not paved at this date but rutted; so that any substantial movement of men and matériel can hardly be conceded away from the main highway, even given the use of pack animals (and/or helots in the case of Sparta).

41. Busolt, 320.

42. Herodotus 5.63.2-5.65.2. Cartledge 146-147.

43. For Sepeia, see Busolt, 332; Cartledge, 149-150; Hooker, 154-5; T. Lenschau, "König Kleomenes I von Sparta" *Klio* 31 (1938) 412-429 (though he opts for the earlier date of 519 B.C.).

44. Busolt, 337.

45. For Agis' campaigns in 418 see Thucydides 5.57-60; Gomme, Andrewes and Dover *ad loc.*; W. J. Woodhouse, The Campaign of Mantinea *ABSA* 22 (1919) 51-84.

46. For the Corinthian War, see Xenophon, *Hellenica* 4.2.9-4.2.18; for Argive-Corinthian unity, Xenophon, *Hellenica* 4.5.1; G. T. Griffiths, "The Union of Corinth and Argos" *Historia* I (1950) 372-386; C. Tuplin, The Date of the Union of Corinth and Argos *CQ* 32 (1982) 75-83; on Iphicrates, see Xenophon, *Hellenica* 4.5.16.

47. On Mantinea II see Plutarch, *Agesilaus* 34; Xenophon, *Hellenica* 7.5.6-7.5.17; Pritchett II, 63-66.

48. A. Demangeon, *Problèmes de Géographie Humaine* (Paris, 1947) 28.

49. J. A. O. Larsen, The Constitution of the Peloponnesian League *C Phil* 28 (1933) 257-276: *C Phil* 29 (1934) 1-19. Cf. 260, "It is safe to conclude that the oracles in question were oaths ratifying treaties."

50. Herodotus 6.74 tr. Rawlinson.

51. A. M. Snodgrass, *Archaic Greece: The Age of Experiment* (London, 1980).

52. Snodgrass, 33; So fortification and urbanization being neither necessary nor sufficient for the advent of the polis are poor criteria for its formation. Will any other serve better? A possible answer lies in the field of religion.

53. Snodgrass, 33, 39, 184, 193.

54. For Pheidon and the heritage of Temenus see A. Andrewes, *The Greek Tyrants* (London, 1956) ch. 3. For Agamemnon at Argos, see Grote, 162-163.

55. J. T. Hooker, *The Ancient Spartans* (London, 1980) 48.

56. The present chapter owes as much to the ideas of Mircea Eliade as its predecessor did to those of Lucian Febvre. The works which have been of immediate use are *The Sacred and the Profane* (New York, 1959); *Patterns in Comparative Religion* (New York, 1958); and *Myth and Reality* (London, 1964); G. S. Kirk in *Myth* (Cambridge, 1970) 5, 7, 255, 257, achieves a caricature of Eliade's thinking.

57. M. Eliade, *The Sacred and the Profane*, 116.

58. *GGR* I, 214, 398-399. For Zeus Lykaios see Pausanias 8.2.1-8.2.3, 8.38.2-8.38.7; Frazer IV, 381-386; *GGR* I, 398-401; A. B. Cook, *Zeus* (Cambridge, 1914) I, 63-99; Eliade, *The Sacred and the Profane* 121-125; *Patterns in Comparative Religion*, ch. 2; A. B. Cook, Zeus, Jupiter and the Oak *Classical Review* 17 (1933) 268-278; A. Brelich, Symbol of a Symbol in J. Kitagawa and C. Long, eds., *Myths and Symbols* (Chicago, 1969).

59. *GGR* I, 398.

60. *GGR* I, 214.

61. Pausanias 8.25.4 (Thelpousa), 8.42.1 (Phigaleia); Frazer IV, 291-292. E. Meyer, in *Neue Peloponnesische Wanderungen* (Bern, 1957) ch. 1 discusses the exact siting of Onkeion by Thelpousa, where the myth in question is set. See, however, P. Levi in *Pausanias: Guide to Greece* (Harmondsworth, 1971) II, 432 n. 179. Levi's first-hand knowledge of the Peloponnesian countryside is reminiscent of the Victorian travellers and no less engaging. See II, 377, n. 25.

62. Frazer IV, 377.

63. C. Lévi-Strauss, *Totemism* tr. R. Needham (Harmondsworth, 1969) 161.

64. Their individuality was still perceptible in 1898 cf. Philippson III.I, 200 In der rauheren Gebirgsluft, in den Tannenwäldern, an den kühlen Bergquellen und den rauschenden Bächen lebten und leben kräftigere und einfachere Menschen...

65. Grote, 82; Eliade, *Patterns in Contemporary Religion* ch. 11; O. Murray, *Early Greece* (Glasgow, 1980) 153-4; R. A. Tomlinson, *Argos and the Argolid* (London, 1972) 201.

66. Pausanias 2.23.6, cp. 2.18.7. For the legendary kings see Pausanias 2.18.3, 2.20.3, 2.22.6, 2.21.3; for the epic cycles see Pausanias 2.18.2, 2.20.4; for the Trojan War souvenirs see Pausanias 2.20.4, 2.22.3, 2.23.1, 2.24.2, 2.22.7; for local heroes see Pausanias 2.20.2, 2.19.4, 2.23.2.

67. For the Argive games see Pindar, *Olympians* 7.83, ὅ τ᾽ ἐν ʺΑργει χαλκὸς ἔγνω νίν. See also the scholia ad loc., Drachmann I, 230-231; ᾽Αρχῖνος ᾽Αργείων γενόμενος βασιλεὺς ὃς καὶ ἀγῶνα πρῶτος

συνεστήσατο, ταχθεὶς ἐπὶ τῆς τῶν ὅπλων κατασκευῆς, ἀπὸ τούτων καὶ τὴν τῶν ὅπλων δόσιν ἐποιήσατο; thus, a national prize, explained in national terms. See also Kirsten-Kraiker I, 345-349, II, 880-881. For the Opheltes story and its connection with the Seven against Thebes see Drachmann, III, 1-5. Tomlinson, 208, comments on the material guise in which Aphrodite appeared at Argos and her connection with the warrior poetess Telesilla.

68. Eliade, *The Sacred and the Profane* 126.
69. O. Broneer, The Apostle Paul and the Isthmian Games *The Biblical Archaeologist* 25 (1962) 2-31 catches the ethos. For Corinth's lack of a legendary past, see L. Malten, Homer und die Lykischen Fürsten *Hermes* 79 (1944) cited by Will, 152 N.4.
70. C. Roebuck, Some Aspects of Urbanization in Corinth *Hesperia* 41 (1972) 100. Will, ch. 3.
71. Will, 187, 192.
72. Plutarch, *Theseus* 25, τελετή; Pausanias 2.2.1; Frazer III, 14-15.
73. For Cyprian Aphrodite see H. Herter in *Eléments orientaux dans la religion grecque ancienne* (Paris, 1960) 61-76; M. Detienne, *The Gardens of Adonis* (London, 1977); Murray, 84-86.
74. For bibliography on the Temple of Demeter and Kore see Wiseman, 15 N.36; for the hierodouleia see Will, 231-233.
75. Forrest, 70-71.
76. See Thomas Kelly in The Traditional Enmity between Sparta and Argos: The Birth and Development of a Myth *AHR* 85:4 (1970) 971-1003 and *A History of Argos* (Ontario, 1976).
77. For Callisthenes see Jacoby, *FGrH* 244 F334.
78. Pausanias 4.22.4 tr. Frazer I, 213; Polybius IV.33.2 has παρὰ τὸν τοῦ Διὸς τοῦ Λυκαίου βωμόν.
79. The commemorative tablet cited by Polybius and Pausanias is a later forgery: see Walbank, *A Commentary on Polybius* I (Oxford, 1957) 481. There might have been an earlier memorial, of course.
80. Plutarch, *Quaestiones Graecae* 39.
81. K. Latte in *PKW* s.v. Steinigung col. 2294.
82. For the Battle of the Fetters see Herodotus 1.66.2; Pausanias 8.47.2, 8.48.2; Frazer IV, 432-436; FGrH 306 F4 (Deinias). For the Spartan defeat at Orchomenus see FGrH 115 F69. For the other two defeats see Polyaenus 1.8 and Pausanias 8.53. Jacoby dates Orchomenus a century earlier.
83. Forrest, 74.
84. Deinias, though late, is explicit on the fact that Perimede/Choira was a queen regnant, not a priestess nor the king's wife: Περιμήδας ἐν Τεγέαι δυναστευούσης. Reigning queens seem to have been regents for minors and localized on the periphery of the Greek world; Artemisia, for example, Penelope, Pheretime of Cyrene. See Chester Starr, *The Origins of Greek Civilization* (London, 1962) 136 for comment and bibliographical notes. PWK has no entry s.v. Königin.
85. For Ares Gynailothoinas see W. Roscher ed., *Ausführliches Lexikon der griechischen und römischen Mythologie* (Leipzig, 1884-1890) cols. 485-486. See J. Gould, Women in Classical Athens *JHS* 100 (1980) 38-59 esp. 57-9, for comment on the exclusion of women in the developed polis.

111

86. The reader may consider Telesilla's defence of Argos an exception. But see now Angelo Brelich, *Guerre, Agoni e Culti nella Grecia Arcaica* (Bonn, 1961) 27. The (aetiological) account given by Socrates of Argos *FGrH* 310 F6 attributes not only the transvestite *Hybristika* to this episode but also the local custom of brides wearing fake beards; therefore, the distinction Brelich (75 N.150) implies between Telesilla's victory (no basis in fact) and Perimede's (un episodio delle secolari guerre tra Sparta e Tegea), is to be accepted.

87. For the bones of Orestes see Herodotus 1.65-68; Huxley, 67-68; D. M. Leahy, The Bones of Orestes *The Phoenix* 12 (1958) 163.

88. Cartledge, 138; Huxley, 68.

89. D. M. Leahy, The Bones of Tisamenus *Historia* 4 (1955) 26-38.

90. For the treaty see Plutarch, *Quaestiones Graecae* 5; F. Jacoby, 'Χρηστούς ποιεῶ' (Aristotle fr. 592 R) *CQ* 38 (1944) 15-16. Aristotle's comment is included by Plutarch in his discussion: ἐξηγούμενος οὖν ὁ Ἀριστοτέλης τοῦτό / φησὶ δύνασθαι τὸ μὴ ἀποκτιννύναι βοηθείας χάριν τοῖς λακωνίζουσι τῶν Τεγεατῶν (fr. 592, Rose).

91. Konrad Wickert, *Der peloponnesische Bund von seiner Entstehung bis zum Ende des archidamischen Krieges* (unpublished dissertation, Erlangen, 1961) 12.

92. See p. 23 supra.

93. For Cleomenes in Arcadia see Herodotus 6.74.1; W. P. Wallace, Kleomenes, Marathon, The Helots and Arkadia *JHS* 74 (1954) 32-35; A. Andrewes, Sparta and Arcadia in the Early Fifth Century *The Phoenix* 6 (1952) 1-5.

94. G. Busolt and H. Swoboda, *Griechische Staatskunde* (Munich, 1926) II, 1320; G. E. M. de Sainte Croix, *The Origins of the Peloponnesian War* (London, 1972).

95. See in addition to the two articles cited in note 57 supra, J. A. O. Larsen, Sparta and the Ionian Revolt *C Phil* 27 (1932) 13-150. R. J. Buck, The Formation of the Boeotian League *C Phil* 67 (1972) 94-101 skirts the issue.

96. Aristotle, *Constitution of Athens* 23.5.

97. Forrest, 89, 91.

98. For Hegesistratus see Herodotus 9.37.4.

99. For the Mantineans at Plataia see Herodotus 9.77 οἱ δὲ ἀναχωρήσαντες ἐς τὴν ἑωυτῶν τοὺς ἡγεμόνας τῆς στρατιῆς ἐδίωξαν ἐκ τῆς γῆς.

100. Snodgrass, 89; Tomlinson, *Argos* 201.

101. For Pheidon see A. Andrewes, *The Greek Tyrants* (London, 1956) ch. 3; A. Snodgrass, The Hoplite Reform and History *JHS* 85 (1965) 110-122; Will, 344-357. See also Strabo 8.3.33 for the Λῆξις Τημένου.

102. Herodotus 9.26.

103. A. R. Burn, *The Lyric Age of Greece* (New York, 1960) 179.

104. For Pheidon and coinage see Will, 347. The post-Heraclid monarchy at Argos may have followed a policy considered Pheidoinian because it tried to impose the Aeginetan standard on former Temenid domains.

105. For Pheidon and Olympia see Pausanias 6.22.2, and Will,

348-9 for the emendation of this passage. The assumption behind the emendation, namely that Hysiae in 669/8 B.C. must precede the Pheidonian anolympiad (revised date 668-664 B.C.), underscores the importance of the highway.

106.   *Anthologia Palatina* 14.73.

107.   For Cenchreae, see Pausanias 2.24.8. L. E. Lord, Pyramids of Argolis *AJA* 42 (1938) 123, rejects this possibility.

108.   J. B. Bury, *The Nemean Odes of Pindar* (London, 1890) Appendix D, The Origin of the Great Games.

109.   For Cleisthenes of Sicyon see A. Andrewes, *The Greek Tyrants* (London, 1956) ch. 5; M. F. McGregor, Cleisthenes of Sicyon and the Panhellenic Festivals *TAPhA* 72 (1941) 266-287. H. Berve, *Die Tyrannis bei den Griechen* (Munich, 1967) I, 27-33; II, 532-535. The description 'Kulturkampf' for Cleisthenes' policy is taken from A. R. Burn, *The Lyric Age of Greece* (New York, 1960) 197.

110.   Herodotus 5.67. τοῦτον ἐπεθύμησε ὁ Κλεισθένης ἐόντα Ἀργεῖον ἐκβαλεῖν ἐκ τῆς χώρης. See W. How and J. Wells, *A Commentary on Herodotus* (Oxford, 1949) II, 34.

111.   For Cleisthenes and the Sicyonian Pythia, Pindar, *Nemeans* 9.9, Drachmann III, 149, 152; for Adrastus' return after the fall of the Orthagorids see Pindar, *Isthmians* 4.26, Drachmann III, 229. See now A. Griffin, *Sikyon* (Oxford, 1982) ch. 2.

112.   Herodotus 5.67; D. M. Leahy, The Dating of the Orthagorid Dynasty *Historia* 17 (1968) 1-23.9.

113.   For Argive-Cleonae relations prior to the transfer of the games to Argos see PWK cols. 2316-2317, 2324 s.v. Nemea, cols. 724-725 s.v. Kleonai; Pindar, frag. 4 Αργεία Νεμέα; Bacchylides 9 v. 11 (Snell).

114.   See supra N. 100.

115.   Busolt, 84.

116.   For the connection between the Dorian state and Apollo Pythaios see Plutarch, *Lycurgus* 6; H. T. Wade-Gery, The Spartan Rhetra in Plutarch Lycurgus VI *CQ* 37 (1943) 62-72.67 N.1; Huxley, 44, 121 N.286; Busolt, 83.

117.   For the Battle of Champions, besides Herodotus 1.82 and Thucydides 5.41, see Chrysermus' account FHG 4 p. 361 Αργείων καί Λακεδαιμονίων|ὑπὲρ|Θυρεάτιδος|πολεμούντων|οἱ Ἀμφικτύονες ἔκριναν πολεμῆσαι ἑκατέρους καί τῶν νικησάντων εἶναι τὴν χώραν...καί τῶν δύο στάσιν ἐχόντων οἱ Ἀμφικτύονες αὐτόπται γενόμενοι Λακεδαιμονίους προκρίνουσι.; also A. Brelich, *Guerre Agoni e Culti nella Grecia Arcaica* (Bonn, 1961) ch. 2.

118.   For Argive losses at Sepeia see Herodotus 7.148 νεωστί γάρ σφῶν τεθνάναι ἑξακισχιλίους; T. Lenschau, König Kleomenes I von Sparta *Klio* 31 (1938) 412-429, 415. Comment has centred on νεωστί rather than ἑξακισχιλίους but Lenschau points out the superiority of Herodotus' total to that of Polyainos' 7777. See also F. Kiechle, Argos und Tyrins nach der Schlacht bei Sepeia *Philologus* 104 (1960) 181-200. 188 N.3.

119.   For the Ambraciot losses see Thucydides 3.113; for Plataia, see Herodotus 9.10 and the discussion in C. Hignett, *Xerxes' Invasion of Greece* (Oxford, 1962) 285; for Athenian hoplite strength in 431 B.C. see Thucydides 2.13.

113

120.   T. Lenschau, König Kleomenes I von Sparta *Klio* 31 (1938) 412-429.418; Herodotus 7.149.

121.   F. Gschnitzer, *Abhängige Orte im griechischen Altertum* (Munich, 1958) 69-81.

122.   Ar. POL. 1303A7.

123.   Plutarch, *de mulierum virtutibus*, 4.

124.   D. Lotze, Zur Verfassung von Argos nach der Schlacht bei Sepeia *Chiron* I (1971) 95-109.

125.   Ar. POL. 1303A34. Cf. Lotze, 97.

126.   Tomlinson, 108 (Mycenae).

127.   For the fines on Sicyon and Aegina see Herodotus 6.92; Busolt 85-86.

128.   For Argive medism see Herodotus 8.73; for the Dorian line-up at Plataea see Herodotus 9.31.

129.   Herodotus 7. 150-152, οὕτω ἂν ὦν εἴημεν ὑμέτεροι ἀπόγονοι, translated by Rawlinson as hereby it would seem that we come of your stock and lineage.

130.   Herodotus 7.148.

131.   Will, 66, 55, 59 N.4.

132.   For the influence of eastern decoration on proto-corinthian ware see J. Boardman, *The Greeks Overseas* (London, 1980) ch. 3, esp. 63, 73. J. Coldstream, *Greek Geometric Pottery* (London, 1968) 331. For the scarabs see H. Payne, *Perachora* (Oxford, 1940) 33-34, 118; for the plaques see Boardman 76; Payne 231-232, 102 nos. 181-183a.

133.   Will, 243.

134.   For Eumelus see Will, 124-129; Roebuck, 100.

135.   T. Dunabin, The Early History of Corinth *JHS* 68 (1948) 59-69; S. Oost, Cypselus the Bacchiad *C Phil* 67 (1972) 10-30.

136.   Will, 239-242.

137.   For Medea, see Will, 81-129; for Bellerophon see Will, 145-168; also, for Bellerophon, F. Schachermeyer, *Poseidon und die Entstehung des griechischen Götterglaubens*, (Berne, 1948) 174. For the cult of Medea at Corinth see Corinth, *Results of Excavations of the American School of Classical Studies at Athens* I.II; H. Stilwell and R. Scranton, *Architecture* (Cambridge, Mass., 1941) 149. For the cult of Bellerophon see Pausanias 2.2.4, Frazer III, 18-19.

138.   M. Eliade, *Patterns in Comparative Religion* (London, 1958) 430.

139.   On Periander and the Isthmian Games see K. J. Beloch, *Griechische Geschichte* (Strassburg, 1912) vol. I.I, 279; Will, 547-548; PWK cols. 2248-2249 s.v. Isthmia.

140.   Will, 547, Périandre n'entendit pas laisser au Sicyonien tout le bénéfice de l'affaire sans lui imposer, sur le terrain même où Clisthène triomphait, et dans un esprit très *agônal*, une riposte éclatante. Eusebius' date for the first Isthmians is 581 B.C., a year after Cleisthenes' *Pythia* (582 B.C.), eight years before the Nemeans (573 B.C.). See now A. Griffin, *Sikyon* (Oxford, 1982) ch. 2.

141.   For Melikertes-Palaimon see Will, 169-180; Farnell, *Greek Hero Cults and Ideas of Immortality* (Oxford, 1921) 39-41; for Sisyphus and

Melikertes see Pausanias 2.1.3. See PWK col. 2248 s.v. Isthmia for versions that omit Sisyphus or replace him with his son Glaukos.

142.   For Theseus at the Isthmus see Drachmann III, 192-193; Plutarch, *Theseus* 25; Will, 191-204. The myth of Actaeon (see Will 180-187; A. Andrewes, The Corinthian Actaeon and Pheidon of Argos *CQ* 43 (1949) 70-78; may be another of these persisting Corinthian hierophanies.

143.   T. Lenschau, PWK col. 1021 s.v. Korinthos.

144.   For the plaque see supra note 132: for the cult of Cyprian Aphrodite see H. Herter, Die Ursprünge des Aphroditekults, in H. Herter ed., *Éléments orientaux dans la religion grecque ancienne* (Paris, 1960). Herter shows that eine Frau maskulinisiert is a Spezialität der kyprischen Religion. For the 'Tavern' see C. Morgan's article A Tavern of Aphrodite *Hesperia* 22 (1953) 131-40.

145.   For Periander's Aphrodite temple in Lechaion see Plutarch *Septem Sapientium Convivium*, 2; F. Imhoof-Blümer and P. Gardner, Numismatic Commentary on Pausanias I *JHS* 6 (1885) 50-101.66; Will, 223.

146.   For the temple of Aphrodite on Acrocorinth see Pausanias 2.5.1; Frazer III, 31-32; *Corinth* III.I, 3.

147.   Will, 231, 233.

148.   K. Steinmetz, *Herodot und Nicolaus Damascenus* (Lüneburg, 1861) cited by Will, 455-456 (cf. 514) and dismissed by him as an amusette de philologue. The vestimentary holocaust (Herodotus 5.92) may have a connection with the difficult passage in John Lydus 4.45, discussed by Will, 232-3.

149.   See J. O'Neill, *Ancient Corinth* (Baltimore, 1930) 100.

150.   See O. Broneer's article cited supra N. 69. For the *arulae* see O. Broneer, Terracotta altars from Corinth *Hesperia* 19 (1950) 591; for Cybele see E. Will, "La Grand Mère en Grèce" in H. Herter ed., *Éléments orientaux dans la religion grecque ancienne* (Paris, 1960) 101.

151.   Snodgrass, 98: a recent discovery suggests that a similar system of artificial tribes, each with members recruited from three geographical districts, existed at Corinth by the mid-fifth century.

152.   The Suidas passage and the fragment of Nicholas of Damascus are closely analysed by Will, 609-615.

153.   G. Busolt and H. Swoboda, *Griechische Staatskunde* (Munich, 1926) I, 363.

154.   S. Dow, Corinthiaca *HSCP* 53 (1942) 89-119; R. Stroud, Tribal Boundary Markers from Corinth *CSCA* I (1968) 233-242.

155.   N. Jones, The Civic Organization of Corinth *TAPhA* 110 (1980) 163-193: an excellent reappraisal of the whole question.

156.   Nic. Dam. fr. 60.

157.   Pindar *O.* 13.6.

158.   C. Meier, *Die Entstehung des Begriffs Demokratie* (Frankfurt, 1970) 25 well characterizes the political experimentation that went on in this century.

159.   See G. Richter, *Engraved Gems of the Greeks, Romans and Etruscans* (London, 1968) 43-44.

160.   *FGrH* 90 F60.

161. E. Norman Gardiner, *Greek Athletic Sports and Festivals* (London, 1910); H. A. Harris, *Greek Athletes ans Athletics* (London, 1964). An interest in twentieth century athletics is the undoing of both authors; see, for example, Harris' concluding chapter. See also p. 200 for an unrepentant gibe at L. Drees, whose books, *Der Ursprung der Olympischen Spiele* (Stuttgart, 1962) and *Olympia*, tr. G. Onn (London, 1968) are among the few serious studies of the ancient games since L. Moretti published *Iscrizioni Agonistiche Greche* (Rome, 1953) and *Olympionikai* (Rome, 1957).

162. Harris, 35.

163. Harris, 53; cf. Gardiner, 20.

164. Harris, 35; Gardiner, 28.

165. 520 B.C.–393 A.D. 520 B.C. marks the introduction of the *hoplitodromos*, the last substantial innovation in the athletic events (Pausanias 5.8.3) while 393 A.D. saw the ending of the games at Olympia.

166. See, for example, Harris, 23-26, 35, 71, and more recently M. I. Finley and H. W. Pleket, *The Olympic Games* (London, 1976).

167. K. Meuli, *Der Griechische Agon* (Cologne, 1968) and Der Ursprung der Olympischen Spiele *Die Antike* 17 (1941) 189-208.

168. Drees, op. cit. N. 74. See also M. Andronikos, *Totenkult* (Göttingen, 1968) 35-37, 121-125.

169. G. Nagy, *The Best of the Achaeans* (Baltimore, 1979) 114.

170. In Meuli's view, the contest allowed Gottesurteil to emerge.

171. E. Vermeule, *Aspects of Death in Early Greek Art and Poetry* (Berkeley, 1979) 62.

172. Typical is hypothesis a. to Pindar's *Isthmians*: ἐτελοῦντο μὲν οἱ παλαιοὶ πάντες ἀγῶνες ἐπί τισι τετελευτηκόσιν. ἐτελεῖτο γὰρ ὁ μὲν Ὀλυμπικὸς τῷ Διὶ διὰ τὸν Πέλοπα, ὁ δὲ Πυθικὸς τῷ Ἀπόλλωνι διὰ τὸν δράκοντα...ὁ δὲ Ἰσθμικὸς τῷ Ποσειδῶνι...εἰς τιμὴν τοῦ Μελικέρτου. Similarly, hypotheses a. and c. to the *Nemeans* describe the contest as ἐπιτάφιος...ἐπὶ Ὀφέλτῃ τῷ Εὐφήτου.

173. J. Coldstream, Hero-cults in the age of Homer *JHS* 96 (1976) 8-17.

174. Murray, 193.

175. W. Burkert, *Structure and History in Greek Mythology and Ritual* (Berkeley, 1979) ch. V, The Great Goddess, Adonis and Hippolytus.

176. R. J. Lifton, *Revolutionary Immortality* (London, 1969). As Lucien Febvre to the first chapter of this study and Mircea Eliade to the second, so is Lifton's psychohistory to the present.

177. Lifton p. IX. See also R. J. Lifton, ed. *Explorations in Psychohistory* (N.Y., 1974) 271-287: The Sense of Immortality: on death and the continuity of life.

178. On the role of the hero in Greek culture see L. Farnell, *Greek Hero Cults and Ideas of Immortality* (Oxford, 1921); A. Brelich, *Gli eroi greci* (Rome, 1958). For a more general survey see C. M. Bowra, *The Greek Experience* (London, 1957) ch. 2, The Heroic Outlook. For the specifically athletic hero see L. Drees, *Olympia* (London, 1968) ch. 9, The Fame of the Victor.

179. Pindar, *N*. 1.69.

180. Lifton, 6.

181. Lifton, XII.

182. Lifton, 7-8. See also R. J. Lifton, *Living and Dying* (London, 1974) 83ff.

183. *GGR* I, 610.

184. M. P. Nilsson, *Greek Piety* (Oxford, 1948) 21.

185. M. P. Nilsson, *Greek Piety* (Oxford, 1948) 29-30.

186. M. P. Nilsson, Mycenaean and Homeric Religion *Opuscula Selecta* II (Lund, 1952) cited by C. G. Thomas, ed. *Homer's History* (New York, 1970) 69-71.

187. L. Farnell, *Greek Hero Cults and Ideas of Immortality* (Oxford, 1921) 95.

188. For Heracles at Olympia see Pindar, *O*. 6.67-70; *O*. 10.24-25, 55-59; Drachmann I, 319-328; L. Farnell, *Critical Commentary to the Works of Pindar* (London, 1932) 82; C. M. Bowra, *Pindar* (Oxford, 1964) 162-164. See also Pausanias 5.8.1 and Frazer III, 484-485.

189. H. J. Rose, *A Handbook of Greek Mythology* (London, 1964) 211-213, 227 N.108.

190. Pindar, *O*. 10.22; ἄπονον δ ' ἔλαβον χάρμα παῦροί τινες. Cf. Farnell's commentary *ad loc.* on χάρμα.

191. Pindar, *O*. 2.

192. Drachmann I, 266.

193. For the nameless Hero see PWK col, 66 s.v. Olympia (Kulte).

194. PWK col. 2521, s.v. Olympia. Cf. PWK col. 65, s.v. Olympia (Kulte).

195. PWK col. 10 s.v. Olympia (Kulte).

196. For the two altars see Pausanias 5.14.5, 5.14.7.

197. Athenaeus 494.

198. For Heracles and the introduction of the olive see *O*. 3.14-17, Drachmann I, 111-112; for the initial sacrificing to Pelops by Heracles see Pausanias 5.13.1.

199. For example, by L. Ziehen in PWK s.v. Olympia, following A. Körte, *Hermes* 39:227. The simplistic thought that Heracles, being Dorian, must postdate the Dorian invasion, underlies this theory.

200. For Heracles in archaic art see F. Bremmer, *Herakles* (Münster, 1953). For the sculpture and painting with Heracles as subject at Olympia see Pausanias 5.10.2, 5.11.2; Frazer III, 423-530, 536-540.

201. PWK col. 18 s.v. Olympia (Verlauf).

202. For a full discussion of the Olympic calendar see A. E. Samuel, *Greek and Roman Chronology* (Munich, 1972) ch. 7. For the archaic Heraea and its relation to the pentaeteris, see PWK cols. 103 s.v. Olympia (Zeit); L. Drees, *Der Ursprung der Olympischen Spiele* (Stuttgart, 1962) 110-118.

203. M. Eliade, *Patterns in Comparative Religion* (London, 1958) ch. 11.

204. For the sacrifices before and after the full moon, see PWK col. 18 s.v. Olympia (Verlauf).

205. This is the original significance of the Olympic Games being ἀγῶνες στεφανῖται, together with the Isthmian, Nemean and Pythian.

117

For the phrase ἱερομηνία cf. for example, Demosthenes 19, 335. For the Olympic truce see PWK cols. 3-6 s.v. Olympia (Gottesfriede).

206.   For the σπονδοφόροι see Pindar, *I*. 2.23, Drachmann III, 218. For the Ἑλλανοδίκαι and their purple robes see PWK cols. 155-157 s.v. Hellanodikai. On Theagenes see Harris, 115-119.

207.   PWK col. 6 s.v. Olympia (Zerlassung).

208.   See L. Drees, *Der Ursprung der Olympischen Spiele* (Stuttgart, 1962) 119-124. For Heracles cf. Macrobius 1.112.28; L. Farnell, *Greek Hero Cults and Ideas of Immortality* (Oxford, 1921) 41, 154, 163.

209.   For the Heraea at Olympia see L. Drees, *Olympia* (London, 1968) 28-30.

210.   Possibly reflected by the traditional date for the introduction of youths' events, 632 B.C.

211.   For a discussion of the time of the festival see Gardiner, 195. Lucian's comment comes from Lucian, *Timon* 4.

212.   For this interpretation of Pindar *O*. 5.6 see Drachmann I, 142. *O*. 5 is dated to 448 B.C.

213.   PWK cols. 2814—2817 s.v. kranz.

214.   Homer, *Odyssey* 8 is describing such an episode.

215.   Drachmann I, 122.

216.   Harris, 47.

217.   The opening twelve chapters of Pausanias' sixth book reflect the mixture of natural and supernatural in the athletic tradition as he found it in his day. Euthymos' and Theagenes' superhuman powers are the most obvious cases of heroic stature being conferred in an athlete's lifetime, but the parallels with Heracles (Polydamas of Skotoussa cf. Diodorus Siculus 13.82) are in their way as significant. Harris' fourth chapter relates many of these stories without appreciating their point.

218.   See L. Drees, *Olympia* (London, 1968) 104-107, 175, where the important reference to Plato's Republic should read 465D not 425D.

219.   PWK cols. 1600-1601 s.v. kranz; M. Blech, *Studien zum kranz bei den Griechen* (Berlin, 1981).

220.   M. Eliade, *The Sacred and the Profane* (New York, 1961) 94.

221.   PWK col. 2531 s.v. Olympia.

222.   Pausanias 5.8.5.

223.   For the ancient writings of the Eleans see Pausanias 5.4.6; Frazer III, 469-470; J. Mahaffy, On the authenticity of the Olympian register *JHS* 2 (1881) 167-178.

224.   For the introduction of these events Pausanias 5.9.1-5.9.2; Frazer III, 487-488.

225.   Gardiner, 71: clearly due to the growing importance of the heavy-armed infantry in Greek warfare. Cf. Harris, 74: A survival of the times when all athletic competition was part of training for war.

226.   For hoplite armour see A. Snodgrass, *Early Greek Armour and Weapons* (Edinburgh, 1964) chs. 3, 5, plates 30-33. See also N. G. L. Hammond, The Campaign and Battle of Marathon *JHS* 88 (1968) 13-57.46 accepting the interpretation of δρόμῳ (Herodotus 6.112) to mean at the double.

227.   A. Snodgrass, The Hoplite Reform and History *JHS* 85 (1965) 110-122.116.

228. Harris, 75.

229. Pausanias 5.9.2; Frazer III, 488; PWK cols. 2814-2817 s.v. Ἀποβάτης.

230. Pausanias 5.9.3 (472 B.C.).

231. T. Klee, *Zur Geschichte der Gymnischen Agonen* (Berlin, 1918) 25. L. Drees, *Olympia* (London, 1968) ch. 7.

232. L. Weniger, Das Hochfest des Zeus in Olympia. II. Olympische Zeitenordnung *Klio* 5 (1905) 1.

233. Gardiner, 52; Harris, 65: Generally in ancient times as in modern it was the shortest race, the stade, which carried the highest prestige.

234. Plato, *Laws* 833A, an interesting passage. Note his retention of *ephippios*.

235. Philostratus, *Gymnastica* 11.

236. Thucydides 3.8, 5.49. See Gomme, *Commentary on Thucydides* (Oxford, 1945) I, 8 N. 3.

237. T. Klee, *Zur Geschichte der Gymnischen Agonen* (Berlin, 1918) 21. Cf. L. Moretti, *Olympionikai* (Rome, 1957).

238. Harris, 105, 106.

239. Pausanias 8.40.1-8.40.2. Cf. Philostratus *Gymnastica* 21; R. H. Brophy, Deaths in the Panhellenic Games: Arrachion and Creugas *AJPh* 99 (1978) 363-390.

240. For a pankratiast's prerequisites see Philostratus *Gymnastica* 35, e.g. ἐποχείσθω δὲ μὴ κενοῖς τοῖς βουβῶσιν, ἀλλ' ἔστω τι κἀκείνων εὐτραφές· οἱ γὰρ τοιοίδε βουβῶνες συνδῆσαί τε ἱκανοὶ πᾶν, ὅπερ ἡ πάλη παραδιδῷ καὶ ξυνδεθέντες ἀνιάσουσι μᾶλλον ἢ ἀνιάσονται. Jüthner comments in *Philostratos, Über Gymnastik* (Amsterdam, 1969), 206, Ein Sieg darin bewies mehr als irgendein anderer die höchste Steigerung der Männlichkeit und machte den Sieger dem Heros der Athleten, Herakles, ähnlich.

241. For the *hippios* race at Nemea see Pausanias 6.16.4. For the character of the *hippios* see J. Jüthner ed., *Philostratos Über Gymnastik* (Amsterdam, 1969) 196. By a pony-tail helmet is meant, e.g. L. Drees, *Olympia* (London, 1968) pl. IX below, nearest runner. Or the race could have been what we call piggy-back. On archaizing at Nemea cf. Philostratos' *Gynastica* 7 δρόμοι δὲ ὁπλῖται παλαιοὶ μὲν καὶ μάλιστα οἱ κατὰ Νεμέαν, οὓς ἐνόπλους τε καὶ ἱππίους ὀνομάζουσιν.

242. Drachmann III, 4-5.

243. See, for example, the arguments of hypotheses b. and c. to Pindar's *Nemeans*, Drachmann III, 2-3.

244. For the Seven against Thebes at Argos itself, cf. note 74 supra; for Aeschylus' *Nemea* see Drachmann III, 3; for Adrastus' brother see hypothesis c. to Pindar's *Nemeans*, Drachmann III, 3; cf. Pindar *N.* 8.52, *N.* 10.28. For Cleisthenes and Adrastus see note 109 supra.

245. For the funerary motif at Nemea see hypothesis d. to Pindar's *Nemeans*, Drachmann III, 4: οἱ κριταὶ φαιὰς ἐσταλμένοι στολὰς κρίνουσι τοῖς ἀγωνιζομένοις ὑπόμνημα τοῦ πένθους ταῖς στολαῖς ἐμφανίζοντες. For funerary celery cf. Plutarch, *Timoleon* 26: τὰ μνήματα τῶν νεκρῶν εἰώθαμεν ἐπιεικῶς στεφανοῦν σελίνας. For Heracles and celery cf. Tertullian, *de Corona* 7.

119

246. C. W. Blegen, Excavations at Nemea 1926 *AJA* (1927) 421-440.
C. K. Williams, *The Temple of Zeus at Nemea* (Princeton, 1966) 27-29.
247. Williams, 27. No trace of any facing was found.
248. See infra N. 261.
249. Gardiner, 225. Cf. hypothesis b. to Pindar's *Nemeans*, Drachmann III, 2: ἠγωνίζοντο δὲ στρατιῶαι καὶ παῖδες στρατιωτῶν · ὕστερον δὲ καὶ ἐπὶ τὸ δημοτικὸν πλῆϑος ἔδραμεν.
250. L. Farnell, *Cults of the Greek States* (Oxford, 1896) I, 63.
251. For the question of a regatta at the Isthmian games see PWK col. 838 s.v. Agones.
252. Gardiner, 214-223.
253. Plutarch, *Theseus* 25; hypothesis b. to Pindar's *Isthmians*, Drachmann III, 192; Will, 199-204.
254. Drachmann III, 194.
255. Will, 169-180.
256. Philostratus, *Heroica* 19.14. Cf. Will, 100 N. 2.
257. See note 188 supra.
258. Will, 210 speaks of an "annéxion des Jeux aux orgia primitifs".
259. See note 141 supra.
260. See note 146 supra.
261. For Attis and the pine tree cf. W. Roscher, *Ausführliches Lexikon der Griechischen und Römischen Mythologie* (Leipzig, 1884) I, cols. 715-727 s.v. Attis. For Attis and the torches see Julian *Orationes* 5, 179B. For Palaimon and the pine tree see Frazer III, 4. For Palaimon and the torchlight worship see O. Broneer, The Apostle Paul and the Isthmian Games *The Biblical Archaeologist* 25 (1962) 2-31.30. For the character of the Pessinuntine mother of the Gods generally see E. Will, Aspects du Culte et de la Légende de la Grande Mère dans le Monde Grec, in H. Herter ed., *Éléments Orientaux dans la religion grecque ancienne* (Paris, 1960) 95-111 and Burkert op. cit. N. 175. It is the motif of the ϑρῆνος which most connects the two; see for Attis, Marinus, *Vita Procli* 33, for Palaimon, Philostratus, *Heroica* 19.14.
262. See note 306.
263. It must be admitted that this innovation is not attested before the early fourth century B.C. See L. Moretti, *Iscrizioni Agonistice Greci* (Rome, 1953) no. 22. For the husplex see O. Broneer, The Apostle Paul and the Isthmian Games *The Biblical Archaeologist* 25 (1962) 2-31, 10-11 and fig. 6. Professor Broneer with great kindness showed the writer how the husplex worked at the Isthmia site.
264. For Pindar and areté see C. M. Bowra, *Pindar* (Oxford, 1964) ch. IV.
265. C. M. Bowra, *Pindar* (Oxford, 1964) 177. Cf. C. M. Bowra, *The Greek Experience* (London, 1957) 21, 95.
266. J. H. Finley, *Pindar and Aeschylus* (Cambridge, Mass., 1955) 7-8. Cf. 40-41, 175.
267. Pindar, *P.* 1.99.
268. L. Farnell, *Critical Commentary to the Works of Pindar* (London, 1932) 10.
269. *N.* 1.69-72.

120

270. *N*. 7.94-101.
271. *I*. 6.47-48.
272. *I*. 6.10-13.
273. This goodwill is shown by the sale at a token price of twenty Corinthian ships to the Athenians for the campaign against Aegina in 487/6 B.C. See Herodotus 6.89.
274. Tod, *GHI*, no. 19; R. Meiggs and D. Lewis, *A Selection of Greek Historical Inscriptions* (Oxford, 1969) No. 27.
275. For 487/6 B.C. see Herodotus 6.89; for 480 B.C. see J. Labarbe, *La Loi navale de Thémistocle* (Paris, 1957) 124; M. Amit, *Athens and the Sea* (Brussels, 1965) 18-21.
276. For the date of Themistocles' *psephismata* see Labarbe, 103.
277. Thucydides 1.14.3.
278. For Corcyra, see Herodotus 7.168; for the Aeginetan total see Pausanias 2.29.5 and Herodotus 8.46; Corinth's total of 40 (Herodotus 8.43 cf. 8.1) has been raised by scholars on the grounds that if there were 40 at Artemision, as Herodotus says, in waters nearer home a reserve fleet will have been added to this number. An Athenian total of 200 is preferred by many: see J. E. Powell, *Herodotus Book VIII* (Cambridge, 1939) 69.
279. See C. Hignett, *Xerxes' Invasion of Greece* (Oxford, 1963) 97 for the suggestion of South Italy as the source of timber for the ship-building program; if this is correct, the Corinthian grip on western trade will have made her ὁλκάδες the likely carriers. See G. Grundy, *Thucydides and the History of his Age* (Oxford, 1948) ch. 14, especially 292: The enormous and sudden increase in the naval strength of Athens introduced a disturbing factor into Greek politics.
280. Thucydides 1.138.
281. For the Ionian total at Lade see Herodotus 6.8: τρεῖς καὶ πεντήκοντα καὶ τριηκόσιαι τριήρεες. For the Thasian effort see Herodotus 6.46.47; they disposed of an income the size of that which the Athenians assigned to shipbuilding in 483.
282. Herodotus 8.3.
283. Herodotus 8.2, tr. Rawlinson.
284. Herodotus 8.5, 8.59, 8.61.
285. See C. Hignett, *Xerxes' Invasion of Greece* (Oxford, 1963) 275.
286. See C. Hignett, *Xerxes' Invasion of Greece* (Oxford, 1963) ch. 5.
287. Herodotus, 8.123-124; Plutarch, *Themistocles* 17.
288. C. Hignett, *Xerxes' Invasion of Greece* (Oxford, 1963) Appendix IX (c). The quotation comes on p. 413.
289. For Adeimantus' son Aristeus see Thucydides 1.60. For the σφοδρὸν μῖσος felt by Corinth after Megara's defection see Thucydides 1.103.
290. Herodotus 8.94. N. Whatley, On the possibility of reconstructing Marathon and other battles *JHS* 84 (1964) 119-139. Whatley's reference to Nicholson's Nek is particularly relevant, one might also compare the variant versions given by participants' contemporaries after Actium.
291. C. Hignett, *Xerxes' Invasion of Greece* (Oxford, 1963) 190.

121

292.　For Timocreon see Plutarch, *Themistocles* 21. For the arbitration in Corcyra's favour see Plutarch, *Themistocles* 24.

293.　Thucydides 1.38; Diodorus 11.70.1; R. Meiggs, *The Athenian Empire* (Oxford, 1972) 51; D. MacDowell, Aegina and the Delian League *JHS* 80 (1960) 119, On the other hand the long-standing friendship between Athens and Aegina's traditional enemy, Corinth, was probably beginning to decline. Herodotus' account of the discussions of the Greek leaders before Salamis indicate disagreement between the representatives of Athens and Corinth, and though it may be exaggerated by later hostility it must have some foundation in fact. See also K. Wickert, *Der Peloponnesische Bund von seiner Entstehung bis zum Ende des archidamischen Krieges* (Erlangen, 1961) 62.

294.　For a discussion of Corinth's agricultural capacity, la riche plaine littorale qui fuit vers Sicyone et, par-delà, vers l'Achaïe (Will, 14) see W. Leaf, *Homer and History* (London, 1915) 210; C. Blegen, Corinth in prehistoric times *AJA* 24 (1920) 10; Wiseman, 9.

295.　Drachmann III, 3, 5.

296.　O. Broneer, The Isthmian Victory Crown *AJA* 66 (1962) 259-263.

297.　Plutarch, *Cimon* 17; E. Meyer in PWK col. 188 s.v. Megara.

298.　(1) G. Busolt, *Griechische Geschichte* (Gotha, 1897) III.I, 260 N. 3. U. von Wilamowitz-Moellendorf, *Aristoteles und Athen* (Berlin, 1893) I, 296 N. 11. (2) See also K. Hanell, *Megarische Studien* (Lund, 1934) 71-73.

299.　E. Meyer, *Geschichte des Altertums* (Basel, 1954) IV.I, 485; G. Hill, *Sources for Greek History* 478-431 B.C., revised R. Meiggs and A. Andrewes (Oxford, 1951) 110.

300.　S. Dow, The Founding and First Century of the Nemea (unpublished paper).

301.　For the speech of the Corinthians see Thucydides 1.41; for the Plataean allusions to past history see Thucydides 3.54, 55.

302.　See note 299 supra. L. H. Jeffery in *The Local Scripts of Archaic Greece* (Oxford, 1961) 162 N. 2 allows a dating range for the lettering of 500-480 B.C.

303.　W. Forrest, Themistocles and Argos *CQ* 54 (1960) 221-241.231 N. 2.

304.　See note 299 supra.

305.　S. G. Miller has published reports of the excavations at Nemea in successive issues of *Hesperia*, beginning 1974. His doubts about the Corinthian presidency are stated in Excavations at Nemea: 1974 *Hesperia* 44 (1975) 149 N. 2; he mentions the rooftiles in the reports of 1979 and 1980.

306.　Hypotheses to Pindar's *Isthmians* b. and c., Drachmann III, 193-194. See also J. Krause, *Die Pythien Nemeen Isthmien* (Leipzig, 1841) 201, N. 13; Plutarch, *Quaestiones Convivales* (Moralia 672D). For Euphorion see PWK col. 1189 s.v. Euphorion. For Procles see Plutarch, *Quaestiones Convivales* 5.3.3. The paraphrase of these sources Plutarch gives concerning the change of crowns in 5.3.3. is significantly worded: ἐκ δὲ Νεμέας κατὰ ζῆλον ὁ τοῦ σελίνου ξένος ὢν ἐπεισῆλθε δι᾿ Ἡρακλέα καὶ κρατήσας ἡμαύρωσεν ἐκεῖνον ὡς ἱερὸν ἐπιτήδειον.

307. Papyrus Oxyrhynchus, Part 18 (1941) no. 2162; H. J. Mette, *Die Fragmente der Tragödien des Aeschylos* (Berlin, 1959) and Nachtrag zu H. J. Mette, Die Fragmente der Tragödien des Aischylos (Berlin, 1959) *Lustrum* 13 (1968) 513-538; B. Snell, Aischylos' Isthmiastai *Hermes* 84 (1956) 1-9.

308. Note the emphasis given to πίτυος by the adverbial καί: You keep an Isthmian festival but with the pine now, not the ivy.

309. The editors of *P. Oxy.* 2162, E. Lobel, C. Roberts, E. Wegener interpret Dionysus' rebuke as levelled at the neglect of their [scil. the chorus'] proper business which is dancing.

310. Papyrus Oxyrhynchus, Part 20 (1952) no. 2256; A. Lesky, Die Datierung der Hiketiden und der Tragiker Mesatos *Hermes* 82 (1954) 1-13.

311. Snell, 8.

312. M. di Marco, Studi sul dramma satiresco di Eschilo *Helikon* 9-10 (1969-70) 373-422.

313. S. Dow, unpublished paper.

314. J..H. Finley, Pindar and the Persian Invasion *HSCP* 63 (1958) 121-132.128.

315. *I.* 8.12.

316. J. H. Finley, Pindar and the Persian Invasion *HSCP* 63 (1958) 121-132.130.

317. *I.* 8.43; νεικέων πέταλα.

318. For the dating of these odes see C. M. Bowra, *Pindar* (Oxford, 1964) Appendix 2.

319. G. Méautis, *Pindare Le Dorien* (Neuchâtel, 1962) 70; E. Thummer, *Pindar, Die Isthmischen Gedichte* (Heidelberg, 1968) 42.

320. For *I.* 2 see C. M. Bowra, *Pindar* (Oxford, 1964) 124-126, 355.

321. For *N.* 4 see C. M. Bowra, *Pindar* (Oxford, 1964) 149.

322. For *O.* 13 see C. M. Bowra, *Pindar* (Oxford, 1964) 144-146; Herodotus I.65.

323. Will, 254.

324. Will, 253.

325. Pindar, fragment 122. See J. H. Finley, *Pindar and Aeschylus* (Cambridge, Mass., 1955) 122: The third strophe slightly apologizes for the poem.

326. For Laïs, see PWk cols. 513-515 s.v. Lais; Pausanias 2.2.4; Frazer III, 19. For Simonides' stanza in praise of the *hierodouloi*, see the scholion on Pindar *O.* 13.326, Drachmann I, 364.

327. See PKW col. 515 s.v. Lais: das Grabdenkmal, (eine Löwin einen Widder zerreissend...) deutet wohl auf ihren Beruf hin: die Löwin war der Aphrodite als der Beschützerin der Hetairen heilig.

328. E. Will, La Grande Mère en Grèce in H. Herter ed., *Éléments orientaux dans la religion grecque ancienne* (Paris, 1960) 99, 101; B. Moreux, Déméter et Dionysos dans la septième Isthmique de Pindare *RÉG* 83 (1970) 1-14, accepting Will's thesis.

329. For Palaimon and the pine tree, see, for example, BMC (Corinth) 75, 78; Frazer III, 4; for Attis and the pine see C. G. Jung, *Symbols of Transformation* (London, 1956) 423 fig. 42; see also D. W. Rupp, The lost classical Palaimonion found? *Hesperia* 48 (1979) 1, 64-72.

330. For Attis and the Attideia in Greece see E. Will, La Grande

Mère en Grèce in H. Herter ed., *Éléments orientaux dans la religion Grecque ancienne* (Paris, 1960) 109, N. 2; *GGR* I, 725; N. Weill, Adoniazousai ou les femmes sur le toit *BCH* 90 (1966) 664-698.

331. Pindar, fragments 79 a and b.

332. For Musaeus see the scholia on Apollonius Rhodios 3.1240 (cited by O. Broneer, The Isthmian Victory Crown *AJA* 66 (1962) 259).

333. For Euphorion see Plutarch, *Quaestiones Convivales* 5.3.2.

334. *Corinth, Results of the excavations conducted by the American School of Classical Studies at Athens* IX; F. P. Johnson, *Sculpture* (Cambridge, Mass., 1951) 47, no. 55.

335. O. Broneer, The Isthmian Victory Crown *AJA* 66 (1962) 259-263.262; S. Dow, unpublished paper; A. B. Cook, *Zeus* (Cambridge, 1914) II, 951, fig. 844.

336. For examples of celery crowns from the Isthmia see the Nicocles Monument IG II^2 3779; IG II^2 3140; the Akhaios Monument, published by M. Mitsos, *AM* 1940: 47-56; all three have celery wreaths. For pine crowns from the Isthmia on reliefs see the Athenaeus Monument (the Hatherton Relief) IG II^2 3145 and the Prometheus herm IG II^2 3767. I owe these references to the unpublished paper by S. Dow mentioned above.

337. A. Brelich, *Guerre Agoni e Culti nelle Grecia Arcaica* (Bonn, 1961) 84. The religious basis of archaic society persisted into the next century. Cleisthenes' ten eponymous heroes, panhellenic outrage at Persian sacrilege (an essential element in the Delian League's formation), the spread of the cult of Athena 'Αϑηνῶν μεδέουσα bear this out. By 431 B.C., as Athens and Sparta exchange accusations of impiety but are in fact jockeying for the better ethical position, the authenticity of the religious motif is paper thin: Thucydides was not the only Athenian to prefer παιδιά καὶ οἶνος to supernatural intervention as explanation for the Hermocopidae. With Socrates' intellectual piety and individual response to *theos* and *cosmos* the curtain is rung down forever on the archaic gemeinschaft. For the state religion of the fifth century see V. Ehrenberg, *The Greek State* (Oxford, 1960) 74-77; for Socrates' true religion, see A. J. Festugière's *Le Dieu Cosmique* (Paris, 1949) chs. 4 and 5. La Lignée socratique.

338. See T. D. Weldon, *The Vocabulary of Politics* (Harmondsworth, 1953) for a discussion of the autarchy of political language. For discussions of Herodotus III, 80-82 see G. Vlastos, Isonomia *AJPhil* 74 (1953) 337-366.337-339; 'Ισονομία Πολιτική in J. Mau and E. G. Schmidt eds., *Isonomia: Studien zur Gleichheitsvorstellung im griechischen Denken* (Berlin, 1964) 3 N. I; M. Ostwald, *Nomos and the Beginnings of Athenian Democracy* (Oxford, 1969) 107, 111-113; C. Meier, Drei Bemerkungen zur Vor- und Frühgeschichte des Begriffs Demokratie in *Discordia Concors* Festgabe für Edgar Bonjour (Basel, 1968) 5 N. 3; *Die Entstehung des Politischen bei den Griechen* (Frankfurt, 1980).

339. For the composition of Herodotus' history see J. E. Powell, *The History of Herodotus* (Cambridge, 1939) chs. 2, 5; C. W. Fornara, *Herodotus, An Interpretative Essay* (Oxford, 1971) ch. 1.

340. F. Bourriot, *Recherches sur la Nature du Genos* (Paris, 1976) 153, 1381-3.

341. Comparable conclusions on the concept of φυλή are to be found in D. Roussel, *Tribu et Cité* (Paris, 1976).

342. H. Erasmus, Eunomia *AC* 3 (1960) 53-64, 63; É. Benveniste, *Noms d'agent et noms d'action en indo-européen* (Paris, 1948) 175.

343. For this definition of *isonomia* see G. Vlastos, Isonomia *AJPhil* 74 (1953) 337-366; also V. Ehrenberg Eunomia in *Polis und Imperium* (Zurich, 1956) 145 (Sparta); M. Ostwald, *Nomos and the Beginnings of the Athenian Democracy* (Oxford, 1969) 64 (Corinth, Solon). For a general discussion of die Bildung eines ersten "nomistischen" Verfassungsbegriffs the reader is referred to C. Meier, *Die Entstehung des Begriffs Demokratie* (Frankfurt, 1970) 15-44.

344. For the Spartan rhetra see A. Andrewes, *Probouleusis*, Inaugural Lecture (Oxford, 1954); for Solon see C. Hignett, *A History of the Athenian Constitution* (Oxford, 1952) ch. 4; for Corinth after the Cypselids see supra ch. 2. For the root νεμ- and its sociological implications see É. Benveniste, *Le vocabulaire des institutions indo-européenes* (Paris, 1969) I, 84, 85.

345. P. Lévèque and P. Vidal-Naquet, *Clisthène l'Athénien* (Paris, 1964) 12.

346. C. W. J. Eliot, *The Coastal Demes of Attika. A Study of the Policy of Kleisthenes* (Toronto, 1962) 147; P. Lévèque and P. Vidal-Naquet, *Clisthène l'Athénien* (Paris, 1964); V. Ehrenberg, Origins of Democracy *Polis und Imperium* (Zurich, 1965) 267; P. Lévèque and P. Vidal-Naquet, *Clisthène l'Athénien* (Paris, 1964) ch. 1 L'espace et le temps civiques de Clisthène.

347. On the demes in the trittyes see D. Lewis, Cleisthenes and Attika *Historia* 12 (1963) 22-40; on κλήρωσις ἐκ προκρίτων see E. Badian, Archons and Strategoi *Antichthon* 5 (1971) 1-34; on ostracism see D. Knight, Some studies in Athenian politics in the fifth century B.C. *Historia Einzelschriften Heft 13* (1970) 1-44.

348. C. Meier, Drei Bemerkungen zur Vor- und Frühgeschichte des Begriffs Demokratie *Discordia Concors, Festgabe Für Edgar Bonjour* (Basel, 1968) 4. For the thesmos/nomos transition see M. Ostwald, *Nomos and the Beginnings of the Athenian Democracy* (Oxford, 1964); for the changing sense of iso — see E. Will's review of Ostwald in *RÉG* 85 (1971) 102-113, an article in its own right; for the recession of the verbal element in νεμ- compounds see H. Erasmus, Eunomia *AC* 3 (1960) 53-64.

349. V. Ehrenberg, Origins of Democracy *Polis und Imperium* (Zurich, 1965) 280. For unmarked as an attribute of concepts, see W. Bakker, *The Greek Imperative* (Amsterdam, 1969) 20. For the Leipsydrion scholion see Aristotle *Ath Pol.* 19. C. Meier, Drei Bemerkungen zur Vor- und Frühgeschichte des Begriffs Demokratie *Discordia Concors, Festgabe Für Edgar Bonjour* (Basel, 1968) 11 N. 27.

350. D. Kagan, The Origin and Purpose of Ostracism *Hesperia* 30 (1961) 393-401, 399; C. Fornara, A note on AΘ.Π22 *CQ* 13 (1963) 1-104, 101. On the introduction of ostracism see G. Sumner, F6 and Ath. Pol. 22 *BICS* 11 (1964) 79-86, D. Knight, Some Studies in

Athenian politics in the fifth century B.C. *Historia Einzelschriften Heft 13* (1970) 21-23. On κλήρωσις ἐκ προκρίτων see E. Badian, Archons and Strategoi *Antichthon* 5 (1971) 1-34; The final quotation comes (again) from V. Ehrenberg's formative "Origins of Democracy" *Polis und Imperium* (Zurich, 1965) 295.

351.   A. Podlecki, The Political significance of the Athenian "Tyrannicide" — cult *Historia* 15 (1966) 129-141.132; E. Vanderpool, *Ostracism at Athens* (Cincinnati, 1970) 8; F. Jacoby, *FGrH* (Berlin, 1926) 328F40 Dritter Teil I, 325; E. Badian, "Archons and Strategoi" *Antichthon* 5 (1971) 8. For the Kritios and Nesiotes statuary see B. Ridgeway, *The Severe Style in Greek Sculpture* (Princeton, 1970) 79-81.

352.   Thucydides 8.48, cf. 3.47.

353.   A. H. J. Greenidge, *A Handbook of Greek Constitutional History* (London, 1914) 204; R. Meiggs, *The Athenian Empire* (Oxford, 1972) ch. 11.

354.   Plutarch, *Themistocles* 21. See also *Plutarchus Themistokles* ed. A. Bauer (Chicago, 1967).

355.   Herodotus 6.83. For the ephebes at Athens see PWK cols. 2737-2746 s.v. Ἐφηβία; cf. Wörrle, *Untersuchungen zur Verfassungsgeschichte von Argos im 5. Jahrhundert vor Christus* (Erlangen, 1964) 105.

356.   W. G. Forrest, Themistokles and Argos *CQ* 10 (1960) 226-228, 238-239. R. A. Tomlinson, *Argos and the Argolid* (London, 1972).

357.   Aristotle, *Politics* 1302B34 -1303A14. The whole passage should be read, for Aristotle is making several points e.g. a similar process, *mutatis mutandis*, can happen in a democracy as the oligarchic faction grows stronger and, secondly, these developments may pass wholly unnoticed (πολλάκις λανθάνει) by both sides.

358.   W.G. Forrest, Themistokles and Argos *CQ* 10 (1960) 240.

359.   PWK cols. 735, 736 s.v. Argolis.

360.   A. H. Greenidge, *A Handbook of Greek Constitutional History* (London, 1914) 215.

361.   See A. Garvie, *Aeschylus' Supplices: Play and Trilogy* (Cambridge, 1969) ch. 1, for the dating of the Supplices to 464/3 B.C.

362.   Aeschylus, *Suppliants* vv. 601, 604; A. Podlecki, *The Political Background of Aeschylean Tragedy* (Michigan, 1966) 62.

363.   Ar. POL. 1302B18; PWK col. 736 s.v. Argolis. E. Badian, Archons and Strategoi *Antichthon* 5 (1971) 1-34.

364.   A. Diamantopoulos, The Danaid Trilogy of Aeschylus *JHS* 77 (1957) 225.

365.   On Pelasgus as a constitutional monarch, see A. Garvie, *Aeschylus' Supplices: Play and Trilogy* (Cambridge, 1969) 150; M. Ostwald, *Nomos and the Beginnings of the Athenian Democracy* (Oxford, 1969) 58, 59; M. Wörrle, *Untersuchungen zur Verfassungsgeschichte von Argos im 5. Jahrhundert von Christus* (Erlangen, 1964) 123.

366.   Herodotus 7.148.

367.   For the occupation, at first peaceful, of Tiryns see Herodotus 6.83; for Mycenae's challenge see Diodorus 11.65. This is to be distinguished from her specific claim to the Nemean Games.

368.   Diodorus 11.54; A. Greenidge, *A Handbook of Greek Constitutional History* (London, 1914) 213-214.

369.   Strabo 8.3.2.
370.   For the Elean inscriptions see G. F. Hill, *Sources for Greek History* (Oxford, 1951) B124. L. H. Jeffery, *The Local Scripts of Archaic Greece* (Oxford, 1961) 218-219, pls. 42-43, is prepared to consider Kahrstedt's dates in the 470's for the relevant inscriptions while herself preferring an earlier date (ca. 500? B.C.) for one of them, her no. 5.
371.   For Mantinea see Strabo 8.3.2; A. Andrewes, Sparta and Arcadia in the Early Fifth Century *The Phoenix* 6 (1952) 1-5.
372.   PWK col. 1319 s.v. Mantinea (Geschichte).
373.   Xenophon, *Hellenica* 5.2.7.
374.   A. Andrewes, "Sparta and Arcadia in the Early Fifth Century", *The Phoenix* 6 (1952) 1-5.3.
375.   On Tegea see Strabo 8.3.; W. Wallace, Kleomenes, Marathon, the Helots and Arkadia *JHS* 74 (1954) 32-35.34 N. 22.
376.   W. Forrest, Themistokles and Argos *CQ* 10 (1960) 229 N. 8.
377.   Polyaenus, *Strategemata* 2.10.3.
378.   R. T. Williams, *The Confederate Coinage of the Arcadians in the Fifth Century B.C.* (New York, 1965); see also the review by J. A. W. Warren in *JHS* 88 (1968) 245-246.
379.   Williams, 13-14; Hiller von Gaertringen in PWK col. 109 s.v. Tegea.
380.   Williams, 15-16.
381.   Williams, 16.
382.   W. G. Forrest, Themistokles and Argos *CQ* 10 (1960) 229.
383.   For the dedication, Hill, Sources B110; for the adherence of Cleonae to Argos see Strabo 8.6.19 (sack of Mycenae).
384.   Diodorus 11.65. Diodorus lists this event under 468/7 B.C. but the context (and use of the imperfect) imply a protracted dispute.
385.   W. Forrest, Themistokles and Argos *CQ* 10 (1960) 227.
386.   Thucydides 1.136.
387.   Aeschylus, *Eumenides* vv. 290, 291; J. H. Quincey, "Orestes and the Argive Alliance" *CQ* 14 (1964) 190-206; cf. *Suppliants* vv. 605-624; W. Forrest, Themistokles and Argos *CQ* 10 (1960) 239-240.
388.   For the siege of Mycenae, see Diodorus 11.65; for the battle of Tegea, see Herodotus 9.35. A. Andrewes, Sparta and Arcadia in the Early Fifth Century *The Phoenix* 6 (1952) 1-5 expounds the Herodotean reference.
389.   W. Forrest, Themistokles and Argos *CQ* 10 (1960) 232.
390.   For Dipaea see Herodotus 9.35; for its date see N. G. L. Hammond, Studies in Greek Chronology of the Sixth and Fifth Centuries B.C. *Historia* 4 (1955) 380-381. Hammond's dating of the outbreak of the Messenian Revolt to 469/8, the hinge of his chronology, has always seemed convincing. See Williams, 26 for an increase in Mantinea coin issues at this time.
391.   Williams, 11, 21, pl. VIII.
392.   Pausanias 7.25.3.
393.   U. von Wilamowitz-Moellendorf, *Pindaros* (Berlin, 1922) 307-310.
394.   Wilamowitz' argument about a reconciliation with Sparta is found in his *Isyllos von Epidauruos* 162.

127

395.   R. W. Macan, *Herodotus, The Fourth, Fifth, and Sixth Books* (London, 1895) I, 341.

396.   See now J. Pollard, *Seers Shrines and Sirens* (London, 1965); L. Farnell, *Cults of the Greek States* (Oxford, 1907) III, 50-62.

397.   For the Common Hearth of the Arcadians see Pausanias 8.53.2 (Tegea) and 8.9.2 (Mantinea); Frazer IV, 212 (Mantinea), 441-442 (Tegea).

398.   For Antinoë see W. Roscher, *Ausführliches Lexikon der Griechischen und Römischen Mythologie* (Leipzig, 1884-1890) col. 379 s.v. Antinoë[3]. See Again M. Eliade on foundations, *Patterns in Comparative Religion* (London, 1958) 392.

399.   A. Diamantopoulos, "The Danaid Tetralogy of Aeschylus" *JHS* 77 (1957) 220-229.

400.   Aeschylus, *Suppliants* vv. 250-259.

401.   Diamantopoulos, 221.

402.   Diamantopoulos, 223.

403.   L. Febvre, *La Terre et L'Évolution humaine* (Paris, 1922) 284, cf. 376: Peu importe de cadre, la marge. C'est le coeur qui vaut.

404.   G. T. Griffiths, The Union of Corinth and Argos *Historia* 1 (1950) 372-386.

405.   M. Sorre, *L'Homme sur La Terre* (Paris, 1961) 333.

BIBLIOGRAPHY

Andrewes, A. The Corinthian Actaeon and Pheïdon of Argos *Classical Quarterly* 43 (1949).
— Sparta and Arcadia in the Early Fifth Century *The Phoenix* 6 (1952) 1-5.
— *Probouleusis*. Inaugural Lecture (Oxford, 1954).
— *The Greek Tyrants* (London, 1956).
— Eunomia *CQ* 32 (1938) 89-102.
Andronikos, M. *Totenkult*, Archaelogica Homerica W. (Göttingen, 1968).
Badian, E. Archons and Strategoi *Antichthon* 5 (1971) 1-34.
Baedeker, Karl. *Greece*[4] (Leipzig, 1909).
Bastide, R. Y a-t-il une crise de la psychologie des peuples *Revue de Psychologie des Peubles* 21 (1966) 8-20.
Bauer, A., ed. *Plutarchus Themistokles* (Chicago, 1967).
Beloch, K. J. *Griechische Geschichte* (Strassburg, 1912).
Benveniste, É. *Noms d'agent et noms d'action en indo-européen* (Paris, 1948).
Berve, H. *Die Tyrannis bei den Griechen* (Munich, 1967).
Blakeway, A. The Spartan Illusion *Classical Review* 49 (1935) 184-5.
Blech, M. *Studien zum Kranz bei den Griechen* (Berlin, 1981).
Blegen, C. W. Corinth in Prehistoric Times *American Journal of Archaeology* 24 (1920).
— The American Excavation at Nemea, Season of 1924 *Art and Archaeology* 19 (1925) 175-184.
— Excavations at Nemea, 1926 *American Journal of Archaeology* 31 (1927) 421-440.
Boardman, J. *The Greeks Overseas*[2] (Thames & Hudson, 1980).
Bourriot, F. *Recherches sur la nature du genos* (Paris, 1976).
Bowra, C. M. *The Greek Experience* (London, 1957).
— *Pindar* (Oxford, 1964).
Braudel, Fernand. *La Méditerranée et le Monde méditerranéen à l'époque de Philippe II* (Paris, 1949).
Brelich, Angelo. *Gli eroi greci* (Rome, 1958).
— *Guerre Agoni e Culti nella Grecia Arcaica* (Bonn, 1961).
— Symbol of a Symbol, J. Kitagawa and C. Long, eds. *Myths and Symbols* (Chicago, 1969).

Bremmer, F. *Herakles* (Münster, 1953).

British Naval Intelligence Division, *Handbook to Greece* (London, 1945).

Broadhead, H. *The Persae of Aeschylus* (Cambridge, 1960).

Broneer, O. Athens in the Late Bronze Age *Antiquity* 30 (1956) 9-19.

—— The Apostle Paul and the Isthmian Games *The Biblical Archaeologist* 25 (1962) 2-31.

—— The Isthmian Victory Crown *American Journal of Archaeology* 66 (1963) 259-262.

Brophy, R. H. Deaths in the Panhellenic Games: Arrachion and Creugas *AJPh* 99 (1978) 363-390.

Buck, R. The Formation of the Boeotian League *C Phil* 67 (1972) 94-101.

—— The Reforms of 487 and the selection of archons *C Phil* 60 (1965) 96-101.

Burn, A. R. *The Lyric Age of Greece* (New York, 1960).

Burkert, W. *Structure and History in Greek Mythology and Ritual* (Berkeley, 1979).

Bury, J. B. *The Nemean Odes of Pindar* (London, 1890).

—— *The Isthmian Odes of Pindar* (London, 1892).

Busolt, G. *Die Lakedaimonier und ihre Bundesgenossen* (Leipzig, 1878).

—— *Griechische Geschichte* (Gotha, 1897).

—— and H. Swoboda. *Griechische Staatskunde* (Munich, 1926).

Cartledge, P. *Sparta and Lakonia* (London, 1979).

Chataigneau, Y. and Sion, J. Pays Balkaniques, P. Vidal de la Blache and L. Gallois, eds. *Géographie Universelle* (Paris, 1934) VII, pt. 2, chap. 36.

Claval, P. Géographie et Profondeur Sociale *Annales, Economies, Sociétés, Civilisations* 22.5 (September-October, 1967) 1005-10046.

Coldstream, J. N. *Greek Geometric Pottery* (London, 1968).

—— Hero cults in the age of Homer *JHS* 96 (1976) 8-17.

Cook, A. B. *Zeus* (Cambridge, 1914).

—— Zeus, Jupiter and the Oak *Classical Review* 17 (1933), 18 (1934).

Cook, J. M. *The Greeks in Ionia and the West* (New York, 1963).

Corinth, Results of the excavations conducted by the American School of Classical Studies at Athens I, pt. I, H. N. Fowler and R. Stilwell, *Introduction, Topography, Architecture* (Cambridge, Mass., 1932).

Corinth, Results of the excavations conducted by the American School of Classical Studies at Athens I, pt. II, R. Stilwell and R. Scranton, *Architecture* (Cambridge, Mass., 1941).

Corinth, Results of the excavations conducted by the American School of Classical Studies at Athens III, pt. II, R. Carpenter and A. W. Parsons, *The Defenses of Acrocorinth and the Lower Town* (Cambridge, Mass. 1936).

Corinth, Results of the excavations conducted by the American School of Classical Studies at Athens VIII, pt. I, B. D. Merritt, *Greek Inscriptions* (Cambridge, Mass., 1931).

Corinth, Results of the excavations conducted by the American School of Classical Studies at Athens IX, F. P. Johnson, *Sculpture* (Cambridge, Mass., 1951).

Corinth, Results of the excavations conducted by the American School of Classical Studies at Athens X, O. Broneer, *The Odeum* (Cambridge, Mass., 1932).

Dawkins, R. M. *The Sanctuary of Artemis Orthia at Sparta* (London, 1929).

Demangeon, A. *Problèmes de Géographie Humaine* (Paris, 1947).

De Sainte Croix, G. E. M. *The Origins of the Peloponnesian War* (London, 1972).

Diamantoupoulos, A. The Danaid Trilogy of Aeschylus *Journal of Hellenic Studies* 77 (1957) 220-229.

Diels, H.; Kranz, W. *Fragmente der Vorsokratiker* (Berlin, 1951).

Dodds, E. R. *The Greeks and the Irrational* (Berkeley, 1963).

Dow, S. Corinthiaca *HSCP* 53 (1942) 39-119.

— The Founding and First Century of the Nemea (unpublished paper).

Drachmann, A. B., ed. *Scholia Vetera in Pindari Carmina* (Amsterdam, 1964-1969).

Drees, L. *Der Ursprung der Olympischen Spiele* (Stuttgart, 1962).

— *Olympia* (London, 1968).

Dunabin, T. The Early History of Corinth *Journal of Hellenic Studies* 68 (1948) 59-69.

Ehrenberg, V. Origins of Democracy *Historia* 1 (1950) 515-548.

— *Polis und Imperium* (Zurich, 1965).

Eliade, Mircea. *Patterns in Comparative Religion* (New York, 1958).

— *The Sacred and the Profane* (New York, 1959).

— *Myth and Reality* (New York, 1963).

Eliot, C. W. J. *The Coastal Demes of Attika* (Toronto, 1962).

— Kleisthenes and the creation of the ten phylai *Phoenix* 22 (1968) 3-17.

Erasmus, H. Eunomia *Acta Classica* 3 (1960) 53-64.

Erbse, H. Anmerkungen zu Herodot *Glotta* 39 (1961) 215-230.

Farnell, O. *The Cults of the Greek States* (Oxford, 1896).

— *Greek Hero Cults and Ideas of Immortality* (Oxford, 1921).

— *Critical Commentary to the Works of Pindar* (London, 1939).

Farrington, B. *Science and Politics in the Ancient World* (London, 1939).

Febvre, Lucien. *La Terre et L'Évolution humaine* (Paris, 1922).

Finley, J. H. *Pindar and Aeschylus* (Cambridge, Mass., 1955).

— "Pindar and the Persian Invasion" *Harvard Studies in Classical Philology* 63 (1958) 121-132.

Finley, M. J. *The World of Odysseus* (New York, 1959).

Flacellière, R. *Daily Life in Greece at the Time of Pericles* (London, 1965) tr. P. Green.

Focke, F. Aeschylos' Prometheus *Hermes* 65 (1930) 259-304.

Fornara, C. W. The Cult of Harmodius and Aristogeiton *Philologus* 113 (1970) 155-180.

Forrest, W. G. Themistokles and Argos *Classical Quarterly* (1960) 221-241.

— *A History of Sparta 950-192 B.C.* (London, 1968).

Frazer, J. G. *Pausanias's Description of Greece* (New York, 1965).

Gardiner, E. Norman. *Greek Athletic Sports and Festivals* (London, 1910).

131

Garvie, A. F. *Aeschylus' Supplices: Play and Trilogy* (Cambridge, 1969).

Gomme, A. W.; Andrewes, A.; Dover, K. J. *A Historical Commentary on Thucydides* (Oxford, 1956-1981).

Greenidge, A. H. J. *A Handbook of Greek Constitutional History* (London, 1914).

Griffin, A. *Sikyon* (Oxford, 1982).

Griffiths, G. T. The Union of Corinth and Argos *Historia* 1 (1950) 372-386.

Grote, George. *History of Greece* (London, 1869).

Grundy, G. *Thucydides and the History of his Age* (Oxford, 1948).

Gschnitzer, F. *Abhängige Orte im Griechischen Altertum* (Munich, 1958).

Hammond, N. G. L. Studies in Greek Chronology of the Sixth and Fifth Centuries B.C. *Historia* 4 (1955) 317-411.

— *A History of Greece to 322 B.C.* (Oxford, 1967).

— The Campaign and Battle of Marathon *Journal of Hellenic Studies* 88 (1968) 13-57.

Hanell, K. *Megarische Studien* (Lund, 1934).

Harris, H. A. *Greek Athletes and Athletics* (London, 1964).

Head, Barclay V. *Catalogue of Greek Coins, Corinth, Colonies of Corinth, Etc.* (Bologna, 1963).

Headlam, J. *Election by Lot at Athens* (Cambridge, 1933).

Henderson, B. *The Great War Between Athens and Sparta* (London, 1927).

Herter, H., ed. *Éléments orientaux dans la religion grecque ancienne* (Paris, 1960).

— "Die Ursprünge des Aphroditekults" in H. Herter, ed. *Éléments orientaux dans la religion grecque ancienne* (Paris, 1960).

Hignett, C. *A History of the Athenian Constitution* (Oxford, 1952).

— *Xerxes' Invasion of Greece* (Oxford, 1962).

Hill, G. *Sources for Greek History 478-431 B.C.* revised R. Meiggs and A. Andrewes (Oxford, 1951).

Holladay, A. J. Spartan Austerity *CQ* 27 (1977) 111-126.

Hooker, J. T. *The Ancient Spartans* (London, 1980).

How, W. and Wells, J. *A Commentary on Herodotus* (Oxford, 1949).

Huxley, G. L. *Early Sparta* (Cambridge, Mass., 1962).

Imhoof-Blumer, F. W. and Gardner, P. Numismatic Commentary on Pausanias I *Journal of Hellenic Studies* 6 (1885) 50-191.

Jacoby, F. *Die Fragmente der griechischen Historiker* (Berlin, 1926).

— "Χρηστοὺς ποιεῖν" (Aristotle fr. 592 R) *Classical Quarterly* 38 (1944) 15-16.

Jeffery, L. H. *The Local Scripts of Archaic Greece* (Oxford, 1961).

Jones, N. The Civic Organization of Corinth *TAPhA* 110 (1980) 163-193.

Jüthner, J., ed. *Philostratos Über Gymnastik* (Amsterdam, 1969).

Kagan, D. Origin and Purpose of Ostracism *Hesperia* 30 (1961) 393-401.

Kelly, T. The Traditional Enmity between Sparta and Argos: The Birth and Development of a Myth *AHR* 75 (1970) 971-1003.

— *A History of Argos* (Ontario, 1976).

Kendrick Pritchett, W. *Studies in Ancient Topography Pt. III (Roads)* (California, 1980).

Kiechle, F. Argos und Tiryns nach der Schlacht bei Sepeia *Philologus* 104 (1960) 181-220.

Kirk, G. S. *Homer and the Epic* (Cambridge, 1965).

— *Myth* (Cambridge, 1970).

Kirsten, E. and Kraiker, W. *Griechenlandkunde* (Heidelberg, 1967).

Klee, T. *Zur Geschichte der Gymnischen Agonen* (Berlin, 1918).

Knight, D. W. Some Studies in Athenian Politics in the fifth century B.C. *Historia, Einzelschriften Heft 13* (1970) 1-44.

Krause, J. *Die Pythien, Nemeen, Isthmien* (Leipzig, 1841).

Labarbe, J. *La Loi navale de Thémistocle* (Paris, 1957).

Larsen, J. A. O. Sparta and the Ionian Revolt *Classical Philology* 27 (1932) 13-150.

— The Constitution of the Peloponnesian League *Classical Philology* 28 (1933) 257-276, 29 (1934) 1-19.

Leahy, D. M. The Bones of Tisamenus *Historia* 4 (1955) 26-38.

— The Bones of Orestes *The Phoenix* 12 (1958) 163ff.

— The Dating of the Orthagorid Dynasty *Historia* 17 (1968) 1-23.

Leake, W. *Travels in the Morea* (Amsterdam, 1968) 3 vols.

— *Peloponnesiaca* (Amsterdam, 1967).

Lenschau, T. König Kleomenes I von Sparta *Klio* 31 (1938) 412-429.

Lesky, A. Die Datierung der Hiketiden und der Tragiker Mesatos *Hermes* 82 (1954) 1-13.

Lévèque, P. and Vidal-Naquet, P. *Clisthène L'athénien* (Paris, 1964).

Lewis, D. M. Cleisthenes and Attica *Historia* 12 (1963) 22-40.

Lifton, R. J. *Revolutionary Immortality* (London, 1969).

— *Living and Dying* (London, 1974).

Lord, L. E. Pyramids of Argolis *American Journal of Archaeology* 42 (1938) 123.

Lotze, D. Zur Verfassung von Argos nach der Schlacht bei Sepeia *Chiron* 1 (1971) 95-109.

Lutz, D. M. The Corinthian Constitution after the fall of the Cypselids *Classical Review* 10 (1898) 418-419.

MacDowell, D. Aegina and the Delian League *JHS* 80 (1960) 118-121.

McGregor, M. F. Cleisthenes of Sicyon and the Panhellenic Festivals *Transactions of the American Philological Association* 72 (1941) 266-287.

Meier, C. Drei Bemerkungen zur Vor- und Frühgeschichte des Begriffs Demokratie in *Discordia Concors. Festgabe Für Edgar Bonjour* (Basel, 1968).

— *Die Entstehung des Begriffs Demokratie* (Frankfurt, 1970).

Meiggs, R. *The Athenian Empire* (Oxford, 1972).

Meuli, K. *Der Griechische Agon* (Cologne, 1968).

— Der Ursprung der Olympischen Spiele *Die Antike* 17 (1941) 189 208.

Meyer, E. *Neue Peloponnesische Wanderungen* (Berne, 1957).

— *Peloponnesische Wanderungen* (Zurich, 1939).

Miller, S. G. Excavations at Nemea, 1974 *Hesperia* 44 (1975).

Mitsos, M. Eine agonistische Inschrift aus Argos *AM* (1940) 47.

133

Morgan, C. A Tavern of Aphrodite *Hesperia* 22 (1953) 131-140.

Moretti, L. *Inscrizioni Agonistiche Greche* (Rome, 1953).

— *Olympionikai* (Rome, 1957).

Moreux, B. Déméter et Dionysos dans la Septième *Isthmique* de Pindaire *Revue des Études Grecques* 83 (1970) 1-14.

Müller, C. and T. *Fragmenta Historica Graecorum* (Paris, 1848).

Murray, O. *Early Greece* (London, 1980).

Mylonas, George E. *Eleusis and the Eleusinian Mysteries* (London, 1961).

— *Mycenae and the Mycenaean Age* (Princeton, 1966).

Nagy, G. *The Best of the Achaeans* (Baltimore, 1979).

Nilsson, M. P. *Greek Piety* (Oxford, 1948).

— Mycenaean and Homeric Religion *Opuscula Selecta* II (Lund, 1952).

— *Geschichte der griechischen Religion* (Munich, 1955).

O'Neill, J. *Ancient Corinth* (Baltimore, 1930).

Oost, S. Cypselus the Bacchiad *C Phil* 67 (1972) 10-30.

Ostwald, M. *Nomos and the Beginnings of the Athenian Democracy* (Oxford, 1969) 228.

Payne, H. *Perachora* (Oxford, 1940).

Philippson, A. *Die Griechischen Landschaften* (Frankfurt, 1959) 7 vols.

Podlecki, A. *The Political Background of Aeschylean Tragedy* (Michigan, 1966).

— The Political Significance of the Athenian tyrannicide-cult *Historia* 15 (1966) 129-141.

Pollard, J. *Seers, Shrines and Sirens* (London, 1965).

Quincey, J. H. Orestes and the Argive Alliance *Classical Quarterly* 14 (1964) 190-206.

Richter, G. *Engraved Gems of the Greeks, Romans and Etruscans* (London, 1968).

Ridgeway, B. *The Serene Style: Greek Sculpture* (Princeton, 1970).

Roebuck, C. Some Aspects of Urbanization in Corinth *Hesperia* 41 (1972) 96-115.

Roscher, W. *Ausführliches Lexikon der Griechischen und Römischen Mythologie* (Leipzig, 1884-1890).

Roussel, D. *Tribu et Cité* (Paris, 1976).

Roux, G. *Pausanias en Corinthie* (Paris, 1958).

Rupp, D. W. The lost classical Palaimonion found? *Hesperia* 48 (1979) 64-72.

Russell, A. G. The Topography of Phlius and the Phliasian Plain *Annals of Archaeology and Anthropology* 11 (1924) 31-47.

Sakellariou, M. and Faraklas, N. *Corinthia and Cleonaea* (Athens, 1971).

Samuel, A. E. *Greek and Roman Chronology* (Munich, 1972).

Schachermeyer, F. *Poseidon und die Entstehung des griechischen Götterglaubens* (Berne, 1948).

Snell, B. Aischylos' Isthmiastai *Hermes* 84 (1956) 1-9.

Snodgrass, A. M. *Early Greek Armour and Weapons* (Edinburgh, 1964).

— The Hoplite Reform and History *Journal of Hellenic Studies* 85 (1965) 110-122.

—— *Arms and Armour of the Greeks* (London, 1967).

—— *Archaic Greece: The Age of Experiment* (London, 1980).

Sorre, Max. *L'Homme sur la Terre* (Paris, 1961).

Stanton, G. The Introduction of Ostracism and Alcmeonid Propaganda *JHS* 90 (1970) 180-183.

Starr, Chester. *The Origins of Greek Civilization* (London, 1962).

Steinmetz, K. *Herodot und Nicolaus Damascenus* (Lüneburg, 1961).

Stroheker, K. Zu den Anfängen der monarchischen Theorie in der Sophistik *Historia* 2 (1953) 381-412.

Stroud, R. The Sanctuary of Demeter and Kore on Acrocorinth *Hesperia* 37 (1968) 299-330.

—— Tribal Boundary Markers from Corinth *California Studies in Classical Antiquity* 1 (1968) 233-242.

Sumner, G. F6 and Ath. Pol. 22 *BICS* 11 (1964) 79-86.

Thummer, E. *Pindar, Die Isthmischen Gedichte* (Heidelberg, 1968).

Tomlinson, R. A. *Argos and the Argolid* (London, 1972).

Tuplin, C. "The Date of the Union of Corinth and Argos" *CQ* 32 (1982) 75-83.

Untersteiner, M. *The Sophists* (Oxford, 1954).

Vanderpool, E. *Ostracism at Athens* (Cincinnati, 1970).

Vermeule, E. *Greece in the Bronze Age* (Chicago, 1964).

—— *Aspects of Death in Early Greek Art and Poetry* (Berkeley, 1979).

Vlastos, G. Isonomia *AJPhil* 74 (1953) 337-366.

—— Ἰσονομία Πολιτική in J. Mau and E. G. Schmidt, (eds) *Isonomia: Studien zur Gleichheitsvorstellung im griechischen Denken* 1-35 (Berlin, 1964).

Wade-Gery, H. T. Eupatridae, Archons and Areopagus *Classical Quarterly* 28 (1931) 1-11.

—— The Laws of Kleisthenes *Classical Quarterly* 27 (1933) 71-104.

—— The Spartan Rhetra in Plutarch Lycurgus VI *Classical Quarterly* 36 (1943) 57-78; *Classical Quarterly* 38 (1944) 1-9, 115-26.

—— *Ancient Society and Institutions* (Oxford, 1966).

Walbank, F. W. *A Commentary on Polybius, I* (Oxford, 1957).

Walker, E. M. *Cambridge Ancient History* (Cambridge, 1927) vol. 5.

Wallace, W. P. Kleomenes, Marathon, The Helots and Arkadia *Journal of Hellenic Studies* 74 (1954) 32-35.

Whatley, N. Reconstructing Marathon and other ancient battles *JHS* 84 (1964) 119-139.

Wardman, A. E. Tactics and Tradition of the Persian Wars *Historia* 8 (1959) 49-60.

Webster, T. B. L. Homer and Attic Geometric Vases *Annual of the British School at Athens* 50 (1955).

Weill, N. Adoniazousai ou les femmes sur le toit *Bulletin de Correspondance Hellénique* 90 (1966) 664-698.

Wickert, Konrad. *Der Peloponnesische Bund von seiner Entstehung bis zum Ende des archidamischen Krieges* (Erlangen, 1961).

Wilamowitz-Moellendorf, U. von. *Aristoteles und Athen* (Berlin, 1893).

—— *Pindaros* (Berlin, 1922).

Will, E. *Korinthiaka, Recherches sur L'Histoire et la Civilisation de Corinthe des Origines aux Guerres Médiques* (Paris, 1955).

—— Aspects du Culte et de la Légende de la Grande Mère dans le Monde Grec in H. Herter, ed. *Éléments Orientaux dans la religion grecque ancienne* (Strasburg, 1966).

—— Review of M. Ostwald, *Nomos and the beginnings of the Athenian democracy*, *RÉG* (1971) 102-113.

Willetts, R. The Servile Interregnum at Argos *Hermes* 87 (1959) 495-506.

Williams, C. K. *The Temple of Zeus at Nemea* (Princeton, 1966).

—— Corinth, 1969: Forum Area *Hesperia* 39 (1970) 1-39.

Williams, R. T. *The Confederate Coinage of the Arcadians in the Fifth Century B.C.* (New York, 1965).

Wiseman, J. *Land of the Ancient Corinthians* (Göteborg, 1978).

Woodhead, A. Ισηγορία and the Council of 500 *Historia* 16 (1967) 129-140.

Woodhouse, W. J. The Campaign of Mantinea *Annual of the British School at Athens* 22 (1919) 51-84.

Wörrle, M. *Untersuchungen zur Verfassungsgeschichte von Argos im 5. Jahrhundert vor Christus* (Erlangen, 1964).

INDEX

Achilles 55
Acragas 80
Acrocorinth 2, 3, 12, 24, 42, 82
Adeimantus 69, 70
Adonis 25, 48, 83
Adrastos 23, 24, 51, 59, 60
Aegina 15, 31, 33, 34, 37, 68, 69,
  71, 72, 74, 80
Aelius Aristides 61
Aeschylus 59, 73, 76–78, 92, 93,
  94, 96, 101, 102, 103
Agamemnon 38
Agesilaus 4, 36
Agis 16, 17
Aietes 40
Aigialeis 35
Aktaion 25
Akte 1, 2
Alcibiades 47
Alpheios R. 27
Ambraciots 36
Andocides 31
Andrewes, A. 108, 109, 110,
  112, 113, 115, 122, 125, 126
Andronikos, M. 116
Antenor 90
Antinoe 102
Aphrodite 25, 42, 62, 82, 83
Apollo 4, 35, 51
Apollodorus 96
Apuleius 42
Arakhnaion 5, 12
Archemorus 51, 59, 60

Archilocus 51
Ares Gynaikothoinas 28
Argolis 2, 4, 20, 35
Argos 1, 2, 4, 5, 6, 8, 9, 10,
  11–13, 14, 15, 16, 23–24, 26,
  27, 32–38, 39, 41, 60, 67, 72,
  73, 74, 75, 76, 81, 86–103,
  104–105
Arion 22
Aristides 42
Aristocrates 27, 47
Aristogeiton 90
Aristomenes 27
Aristotle 37, 92, 94
Arkadia 1, 6, 7, 8, 11, 14, 18,
  20–22, 26–28, 29, 30, 31, 32,
  38, 41, 98, 99, 100, 101, 102,
  104
Arnold, T. 47
Arrichion of Philageia 58
Artemision 71
Asine 15
Asopus 6, 9
Aspis 24
Athamas 61
Athena 23, 28, 83
Athenaeus 4, 82
Athens 11, 16, 28, 36, 43, 44,
  61, 67–70, 71, 72, 74, 77, 79,
  84, 86–91, 92, 93, 94, 96, 101,
  102, 103
Attis 48, 63, 83, 84
Ayionorion 4, 5

137

138

139

Thummer, E. 123
Thyamia 9
Thyestes 23
Timasarchus 80
Timocreon 71, 91
Tiryns 12, 35, 38, 95, 100, 101
Tisamenus of Elis 29, 100
Titane 9
Tomlinson, R. 109, 110, 111,
    112, 114, 126
Tretus 17
Trikaranon 6
Tripolis 11
Troezen 33, 36, 38
Tuplin, C. 109
Tyrtaeus 56

Vanderpool, E. 126
Vermeule, E. 109, 116
Vlastos, G. 124, 125
Vytina 13

Wade-Grey, H. 113
Wallbank, F. 111
Wallace, W. 112, 127
Weill, N. 124
Whatley, N. 121
Wickert, K. 112, 122
Wilamowitz-Moellendorf, U. von
    122, 127
Will, E. 107, 111, 112, 114, 115,
    120, 123, 125
Williams, C. 120
Williams, R. 127
Wiseman, J. 108, 111, 122
Woodhouse, W. 109
Wörrle, M. 126

Xenocrates 80
Xenophon 6, 17, 31, 81, 82,
    109, 127
Xerxes 38, 68

Zeus 21, 27, 84, 100